Praise for *Blaze Your Own Trail*

"The intrapersonal journey described in this book gives the reader insight into the world of choice, especially for women who are working to find or create balance in their personal and professional lives. The stories shared in this work encompass the challenge we all have as human beings in wondering 'what if?' in our daily lives. This book will have an impact on the perspectives we hold when evaluating our privileges and struggles. It brings to life the reality that our journeys are multidimensional and that the dimensions are defined by our identities,decisions, and the actions of others. It is intriguing how the author speaks to readers as if they are directly experiencing the events taking place in the book, making the realities felt through the character's thoughts relatable and powerful."
—Cheryl Ingram, founder and CEO, Diverse City LLC

"*Blaze Your Own Trail* provides valuable insight into the experiences and choices that a woman makes in her life, beyond what many of us might be aware of. As a tech CEO and an investor, as well as a father and husband, I have long recognized the role I need to play in empowering women in their careers. The insight I have gained from this book has helped me feel more empathy around many of the obstacles that I wasn't even aware of and has inspired me to be a more effective ally."
—Spencer Rascoff, cofounder of dot.LA, Zillow, and Hotwire

"If you think this is some stranger's story, think again. At every crossroads, I found myself on the path of a woman I know and love—confronting her choices, facing her struggles, and embracing her hope. We grow up thinking that the wrong twists and turns could ruin everything. But we are way too strong for that."
—Mónica Guzmán, cofounder of The Evergrey

"Every once in a while, an author so delightful and smart breaks through with a winning idea for the world. With interactive, useful, and fun-to-read chapters like 'Love or Marriage,' 'Ladder or Jungle Gym,' or 'Snot and Tears,' *Blaze Your Own Trail* walks us through career and life choices with poignancy and power. In what is one of the most emotionally fraught topics of today's age—gender equity in the office and home—Rebekah manages to provide a winning framework for anyone giving big life decisions full consideration. A must-read for everyone, male or female, parent or child. I loved it!"

—Jonathan Sposato, Chairman, GeekWire, and author of *Better Together*

"Rebekah distills the defining moments of life—excitement, choices, hardships—into interactive, fun-to-read chapters that offer a glimpse into every woman's reality. She intersperses the story with grounding statistics on themes like choosing a career, motherhood, workplace harassment, relationships . . . and the result is a book that feels reassuring, kind, and comforting for any woman who has ever had a decision to make. A wonderful and refreshing reminder that, even when everything feels out of our control, we are the creators of our story."

—Amy Nelson, founder and CEO, The Riveter

BLAZE YOUR OWN TRAIL

BLAZE YOUR OWN TRAIL

An Interactive Guide to Navigating Life with
Confidence, Solidarity, and Compassion

REBEKAH BASTIAN

Berrett–Koehler Publishers, Inc.

Berrett-Koehler Publishers, Inc.
1333 Broadway, Suite 1000
Oakland, CA 94612-1921
Tel: (510) 817-2277
Fax: (510) 817-2278
www.bkconnection.com

ORDERING INFORMATION

Quantity sales. Special discounts are available on quantity purchases by corporations, associations, and others. For details, contact the "Special Sales Department" at the Berrett-Koehler address above.

Individual sales. Berrett-Koehler publications are available through most bookstores. They can also be ordered directly from Berrett-Koehler: Tel: (800) 929-2929; Fax: (802) 864-7626; www.bkconnection.com.

Orders for college textbook / course adoption use. Please contact Berrett-Koehler: Tel: (800) 929-2929; Fax: (802) 864-7626.

Distributed to the U.S. trade and internationally by Penguin Random House Publisher Services.

Berrett-Koehler and the BK logo are registered trademarks of Berrett-Koehler Publishers, Inc.

Printed in the United States of America.

Berrett-Koehler books are printed on long-lasting acid-free paper. When it is available, we choose paper that has been manufactured by environmentally responsible processes. These may include using trees grown in sustainable forests, incorporating recycled paper, minimizing chlorine in bleaching, or recycling the energy produced at the paper mill.

Library of Congress Cataloging-in-Publication Data
Names: Bastian, Rebekah, author.
Title: Blaze your own trail: an interactive guide to navigating life with
    confidence, solidarity, and compassion / Rebekah Bastian.
Description: First edition. | Oakland, CA: Berrett-Koehler Publishers,
    [2020] | Includes bibliographical references.
Identifiers: LCCN 2019030613 | ISBN 9781523087952 (paperback) | ISBN
    9781523087969 (pdf) | ISBN 9781523087976 (epub)
Subjects: LCSH: Life change events. | Women--Psychology. | Individuality. |
    Plot-your-own stories.
Classification: LCC BF637.L53 B37 2020 | DDC 155.3/339--dc23
LC record available at https://lccn.loc.gov/2019030613

First Edition
27 26 25 24 23 22 21 20 19   10 9 8 7 6 5 4 3 2 1

Book producer and text designer: Happenstance Type-O-Rama
Cover design and illustration: Yvonne Chan
Interior illustration: Yvonne Chan

Dedicated to my husband, Shane:
I am thankful for the many
decisions that have resulted in
the life we share and for the
support and inspiration that
you fuel me with.

CONTENTS

CONTENTS

CONTENTS

THE DECISION TREE

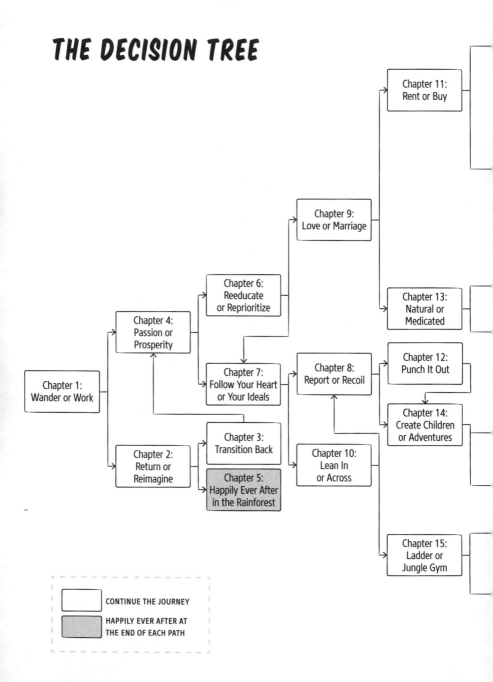

Chapter 1:
Wander or Work

Chapter 2:
Return or
Reimagine

Chapter 4:
Passion or
Prosperity

Chapter 3:
Transition Back

Chapter 5:
Happily Ever After
in the Rainforest

Chapter 6:
Reeducate
or Reprioritize

Chapter 7:
Follow Your Heart
or Your Ideals

Chapter 9:
Love or Marriage

Chapter 8:
Report or Recoil

Chapter 10:
Lean In
or Across

Chapter 11:
Rent or Buy

Chapter 13:
Natural or
Medicated

Chapter 12:
Punch It Out

Chapter 14:
Create Children
or Adventures

Chapter 15:
Ladder or
Jungle Gym

CONTINUE THE JOURNEY

HAPPILY EVER AFTER AT
THE END OF EACH PATH

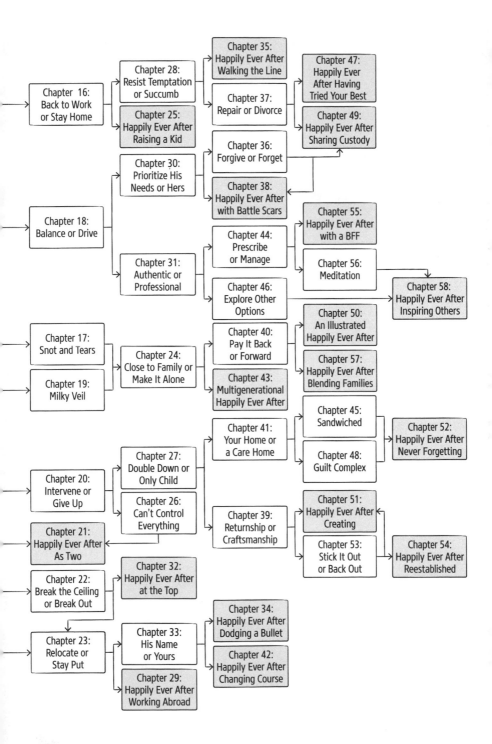

FOREWORD

"*I*f you could go back in time and say anything to your younger self, what would it be?"

The first time I was asked this question I was on stage during a conference. I was thirty-five years old, married, seven months pregnant with my first child, had just spent forty weeks traveling through the emerging world for my second book, and had been promised a massive promotion at work.

I had already faced a lot of the dilemmas that the protagonist of this book faces in the pages to come. I'd put off having kids. I'd called off one wedding that didn't feel quite right at the last minute. I'd decided not to change my name when I did finally get married. I'd refused higher paying jobs to do what I was passionate about. That book on emerging markets, for instance, had cost me hundreds of thousands of dollars in travel expenses and opportunity cost to write. But after it published, I'd gone to five continents promoting it and done speaking gigs all over the world—all while pregnant—and in the process, I more than made that money back.

I was happy. The risks had paid off, the tradeoffs all felt worth it. I felt a rare sense of peace wash over me, and I answered, "I would tell the younger me to calm down. *It's all going to work out fine.*"

That would have been a big ask of the younger me. I still vividly remember the anxiety I had in my teens and early twenties over my future: Would I ever fall in love? Would I ever find someone who could appreciate me? What on earth was I qualified to do for a living? Did I want to be a mom? Would becoming a mom require me to throw away everything I'd ever worked for?

What a waste of all that stress, I thought that day when I was asked the question. *It was all fine.*

Since that moment, I've had two kids, I've started two companies, I've gotten divorced, that promotion I was promised got handed to a dude while I was in labor, I've been hospitalized from over-work, I've had threats made against my family, I got kidnapped in Nigeria and had to bribe my way out, and I once had a repo guy show up for my minivan.

But guess what? Although many of those moments felt like the end of the world at the time, it has still somehow *all worked out fine.* I'm in a loving relationship, I've started a company called Chairman Mom that makes working women's lives better on a daily basis, my kids are phenomenal, I'm healthy, and I have more girlfriends than I did in college.

Young women face an uncertain, unfair, and legitimately scary world. But young women are also amazingly resourceful, adaptable, and resilient.

Spoiler: In the amazing adventures you are about to go on in this book, it will also *all work out fine,* no matter what path you take. There are nineteen different happy endings with a pretty big range of outcomes. The delicious part of this book is that it gives you what real life can't: it allows you to compare your happy endings and reexamine the paths that got you there. It gives you dozens of do-overs.

You don't have to sit and watch while the protagonist stays in a relationship that creeps you out, or a job that isn't fulfilling, or when she makes a choice you wish she hadn't. You make the decisions for her. You can see what it's like to make the choices you never would in real life, consequence-free.

The protagonist ends each version of her story feeling fulfilled, happy, and like *it all worked out fine,* even though the endings aren't all equally happy. Part of what's stunning about this book, is that it explores the subjectivity of what a happy ending is.

Some women may find Chapter 50 to be one of the worst ways to end their story. I found it one of the best. It's not only subjective to who you are, it's subjective based on what stage you are at in your life. This is a book you can revisit ten years after you first dive in, curious to see if your choices change now that your own bets have played out.

In my own life, I can look back and see the different forks I took and imagine how my happy endings might be different had I taken a different path.

I work in the startup industry, where the odds of success are daunting: even though 68 percent of business owners in America are women, we only get 2 percent of the venture capital invested each year. I've largely been able to beat those odds because of who I knew, which was based on a series of forks I took in the road. Different forks, and I might not be running my own multimillion-dollar company right now.

Women experience a lot of pressures in their lives to choose the "right" path, and often times it feels like the right path was the one we didn't take. We bear the motherhood penalty if we decide to have kids, or we push against societal norms if we don't. We feel judged whether we work or we stay home, with nearly 90 percent of women witnessing "mom shaming." And this is to say nothing of the heartbreaking ubiquity of sexual harassment and sexual assault exposed by the #MeToo movement, with a double-edged sword of choices for how to respond.

All of this ratchets up the fear of making the wrong move. It's true that the moves you make matter, and small things could impact what you do, where you live, and who you are with. But somehow, because women are so strong, so resourceful, and so resilient, it will *all still work out fine.*

Sometimes I shudder when I think about the near misses in my own life. What if I had married the first man I was engaged to? What if I hadn't gotten out of my home town? What if I had decided not to have kids? What if I put money before passion any of the dozens of times I wrestled with that very choice? There's a duality in these questions that is as comforting as it is unsatisfying.

As you map this book against your own experience, you can begin to compare the outcomes to your own happy endings. The more we share our real-life struggles and decision points and are grateful for our own happy endings, the more we can appreciate the fullness of the choices we made, understand the choices of others, and recognize the things that were outside our control.

As you see the protagonist's journey unfold, and as you see your own choices mirrored in various paths, you can begin to feel the confidence that *it is, in fact, all going to work out fine.*

—SARAH LACY
Author of *A Uterus Is a Feature, Not a Bug* and CEO of Chairman Mom

PREFACE

My conscious mind didn't come up with the idea for this book. Rather, I shot awake at 3:30 A.M. with the idea in my head. That phenomenon is not entirely new to me—I've been woken by crazy ideas many nights—but the difference with this one was that I wasn't able to talk myself out of it. Somehow all of the expectations, trials, challenges, heartbreaks, and triumphs that I ever knew women to go through—my own, those of my close friends, and those of the countless women that I've had the privilege of getting to know professionally—cried out to me to write this book.

I have the benefit of being a living example of crooked paths, magnificent screw-ups, and shocking successes. Perhaps that in itself qualifies me to write about the unpredictability of our choices and the survivability of our crashes. On top of that, I've been lucky to have the close bonds of friendship that have allowed me to live multiple lives at once. My friends and I have experienced each other's emotions as though they were our own—we have laughed, cried, raged, and celebrated together.

When I first started out on my professional journey—a bit later than many due to that crooked path I mentioned—I had the level of arrogance that is often expected and somewhat endearing in a young woman. Yes, I had heard the stories about being a woman in the workplace—and specifically a woman in tech in my case—and about the challenges that come with different life stages. But I was strong and smart, and I wasn't going to put up with any shit. I'd avoid the pitfalls.

As I moved into higher levels of leadership, I started hearing the stories of other women more and more—women would reach out for mentorship, confide in me about issues they were having, or even just tell me stories of past jobs and life experiences. As I became privy to more of these experiences, I started to understand a few things. And I started to feel the urgency to share these ideas with others.

1. So many women enter the career phase of their lives believing that they're supposed to know where they're going and that there is one right path to follow to get there. This belief is dangerous because it sets us up for disappointment, for feelings of failure, and, worst of all, it can close our eyes to opportunities we never imagined. We need to throw away this idea and feel confident without knowing exactly where we're headed.

2. We go through a lot of challenges in our lives that don't get talked about much. Some are our own faults, some are just bad luck. But because of the taboo nature of these events, we end up feeling like we're the only ones going through them. We're not! By talking with each other about these raw, vulnerable experiences, we can recognize that we're not alone, feel the strength of the many women who have gone through similar obstacles, and let ourselves experience comfort in that solidarity.

3. We never fully know what someone else is going through—especially if that someone is outside our circle of closest friends. When we embrace that fact, we can assume the best about others and feel compassion and empathy for the journey that they are on.

I haven't gone through every decision or outcome in this book myself, so I am grateful to the many women who have shared their journeys with me so I could compile an experiential glimpse into the infinite paths our lives can take. In addition to the anecdotal research that went into this, I have also woven data into the plot lines to help quantify the frequency and probability of many of these experiences.

There are nineteen different endings and many more combinations of paths to discover in this book. My hope is that you will explore multiple journeys—to better understand the many experiences a woman might go through, and because...when else do you get to go back in time and redo a decision?

I hope you walk away from this book feeling more confident in blazing your trail without knowing exactly where it is going, that you experience solidarity by realizing how many of us are persevering through similar challenges, and that you build compassion for the journeys that we are all on.

PROLOGUE

You've come a long way, lady. And you have so much ahead.

At the start of this book, you are a young woman setting out on the many experiences, decisions, and pathways of your adult life. You begin this journey as you end your last journey—that of your childhood and college years. Some of the choices that lie ahead are more predictable: those high-level decisions that surround your career, the partner you choose, and motherhood. Those are the ones you've heard the most about. But as you live the actual effects of each of your decisions, you'll find that choices emerge for you that are rarely talked about and much more nuanced. And every decision you make—large or small—will affect your ultimate life path.

How this journey unfolds is up to you. There are many ways through this literary life-journey and many happy endings. Happy, not because they're all fairytale endings, but because you will find that, ultimately, regardless of your struggles, you will push through, that you are strong, and that you will be ok. Even better, you have a unique advantage: while living in the pages of this book, you can turn back decisions and try another route. Don't get too used to that, though.

Perhaps this journey through your 20s and 30s as a young woman will be very close to the reality you will experience when you close this book. These choices can be comforting both in their similarity to your own life and in the power they offer you to think through what lies ahead.

Or maybe this book will be your first plunge into experiencing a world that views you as a young woman if that is not an identity that you currently express. If this is the case, you can look forward to exploring new perspectives gaining a deeper understanding of the life that you don't generally get to live, and you can come out of it with new empathy and appreciation for what a woman may experience and perhaps some of what your future may hold.

In the coming journey, you are a college-educated, able-bodied, heterosexual white woman. So in many regards, you are already starting from first (if not second or third) base. If you were to experience the journey of a young Black, Latina, or Queer woman, or that of a woman with a mental or physical disability—to name just a few examples—the choices that you would have open to you and the decisions you would need to make could look vastly different. But at the same time, the experiences that will unfold in this journey are shared by many women, and in these pathways, we can find solidarity.

Everyone's path is different, and everyone is a result of both the social systems that surround them and their own actions.

Now sit down and hold on—your journey is about to begin.

1

WANDER OR WORK

Congratulations! The world is your oyster. You're in your final days of a dual communications and math degree, you're 99.2 percent certain to get your diploma (pending one linear algebra exam . . . it's probably fine), and you have choices laid out in front of you. Sure, you may only end up making eighty-two cents for every dollar that Andy—your on-again-off-again boyfriend—will make, but you have an amazing group of friends, big aspirations for making the world a better place, and a heart that has never been broken—you are ready to take life by the horns.[1]

Getting out of college isn't quite as liberating or optimism-inducing as you remember high school graduation being—then, you were finally able to leave your insecurities, quarreling parents, and spotted reputation behind—but it does seem like you have less baggage to shrug off from your 4.25 university years. Sure, you might have had an embarrassing public breakup, some common-room-vomit your freshman year, and a couple of exhausted meltdowns (mostly among friends). But those were pretty par for the course, and you feel like you won't need to fully reinvent yourself in this next phase of life.

That said, there have been an uncharacteristic number of pep talks in your life lately. There was the, admittedly, moving pre-graduation speech from the alumni who started his own global shipping company. Then the slightly less moving—but more predictable—lecture from your mom about paying back student loans and using birth control (the latter probably would have been more timely seven years ago). And finally, the most exciting (and most buzzed) "pep talk" from your BFF about the possibilities ahead. "Who rules the world?!"

Those upcoming possibilities, while exciting, are actually pretty daunting in their limitlessness. It's not completely lost on you—based on the Socioeconomics 101 class you took your freshman year and the Racial Anthropology series you conquered as a sophomore, not to mention the daily news cycle—that the mere fact that you have so many options is a result of privilege.

The idea that you're privileged was actually pretty counterintuitive to you the first time you encountered it; you felt like you'd had your share of struggles already handed to you. From your parents' constant fighting (and eventually divorce) to a ten-month bout with an eating disorder, to that asshole who sent you into a shame spiral after groping you at your high-school senior year prank night. And the fact that you had to work at gigs like Pizza Mart and Toy Time since you turned sixteen (and were babysitting even before that) just to buy the outfits that would stave off ridicule. You wouldn't have chosen *privileged* as one of the words to describe yourself.

But fortunately, you're of a slightly more enlightened generation than even your aunt Ashley's (although she is only ten years older), and you're days away from a liberal arts degree. So you now understand that the options that span out in front of you might not have been so expansive if you had experienced the systems of oppression that many of your classmates—and

4

even more so, those who didn't end up at this second-tier, yet respectable, college—have had to live with. You recognize that, and you really want to "be the change" that dismantles those systems.

But first you want to celebrate graduation in your new party ensemble! And then you need to figure out where you're going to be living next month.

Your boyfriend Andy (or is that even too gracious a title for someone who makes time to make out, but only when other more exciting plans don't come up?) is heading to law school on the East Coast in the fall. You have no interest in more school at this point, and he's not exactly making the case for following him, so that option is off the table.

Your BFF Sam has been bitten by wanderlust and is trying to talk you into traveling the world with her. Honestly, that sounds amazing, and you know that the number of college graduates who take a gap year before starting in on real life is on the rise, so crazier things have definitely happened. And you know there are some opportunities for teaching or working shorter term jobs, so it is not like you would be entirely without income while seeing the world.

At the same time, the combination of your college debt and an unexplainable urge to prove yourself as some kind of "career woman" (although that title only makes you think of bad 90s businesswoman dramas!) is whispering in your other ear. Even with some sort of job internationally, you wouldn't be paying down the loan principle at all, and so you would be coming back to even more debt to climb out of. There's a career fair on campus tomorrow and a stack of edited resumes on the peeling Ikea desk in your apartment.

There is no universal right answer here. In a recent survey, the paths out of college were pretty evenly split: 35 percent of people jump straight into their career after college, 32 percent take up to five years to get their career started, and 33 percent spend closer to ten years—or more—getting going.[2] The average new graduate spends 7.4 months looking for their first job.[3]

Sam pops in just as you're contemplating. "Want to grab a drink, spin a globe, and figure out where to jet off to, girl?"

If you decide to blow off the career fair, make travel plans with Sam, and invest in a little worldly learning, despite the fact that it will add to your already-growing debt, turn to **Chapter 2.**

If you don't feel that world travel is a viable option, decide to get a good night's sleep so you can do some shiny-eyed resume pushing tomorrow, and get your dream job and your finances in order ASAP, turn to **Chapter 4.**

2

RETURN OR REIMAGINE

You wake up to the sound of Howler monkeys. Even after seven weeks of this alarm clock, the barking howl still takes you by surprise. You and Sam have been staying with neighboring host families in a small town in southeastern Costa Rica and have been teaching English and math at the local elementary school through a year-abroad teaching fellowship. It pays very little, but for the moment, it's just enough to make ends meet.

Of course, this is doing almost nothing to address your student loan debt and not much more than that to build the experience that you anticipate will be relevant to your career. But you're having the most fun and eye-opening experience you have ever had.

With daily practice to improve your rusty high-school Spanish, along with the training that the volunteer abroad program provided, you feel equipped to teach the eight-to-twelve-year-olds in your classroom. And yet you can't help wonder who is really benefiting the most from this experience. As you watch a fellow volunteer take selfies with some of the children, you feel a pang of embarrassment over the white savior complex that could be derived from this experience. You try to push that guilt away and make the most of your days, because the children you work with are the best part of it.

In the evenings, you and Sam often ride rusty, single-speed bicycles down the dirt road into town and go dancing at one of the reggae bars. It is on one such night that you end up chatting with a local gentleman named Eddie. He's from Argentina, but lives in Puerto Viejo now, and is doing research on the mating habits of sea turtles. You hit it off instantly, talk into the night and, after a short, but heart-stopping good-night kiss, agree to meet for a beach hike the coming weekend.

Thus begins your Costa Rican romance. You slowly find yourself spending more and more of your free time with Eddie. Even though you are both foreigners, your budding relationship with him makes you feel even more connected to your new locale.

Unfortunately, the relationship is having the opposite effect on your friendship with Sam. She is bummed that Eddie is getting so much of your time and completely sick of hearing about him when you two are together. You assume that is a large part of the reason that, at the turnover of semesters at the elementary school, she announces that she's going to head to Argentina to volunteer on an organic farm. She half-heartedly asks if you'd like to join her, but you both already know the answer.

And so you go through the next five months in your enjoyable new reality. Teaching children by day, eating occasional meals with your host family—they are an older couple whose children are grown and they enjoy your company but don't expect it—and spending the rest of your time exploring both land and mind with Eddie.

Before you know it, your year-abroad program is coming to an end. That means that your teaching gig, work visa, and host family accommodations will be ending soon. On the afternoon of your twenty-third birthday, you and Eddie have a picnic on the beach and discuss the options in front of you.

If you were to stay in this village, there wouldn't be much to do career-wise. You might be able to get hired as a full-time teacher at the school where you've been working, but, as much as this experience has been fulfilling and eye-opening for this finite amount of time, you can't see yourself teaching the same lessons over and over again. And, although your feelings for Eddie are as close as you've ever come to being madly in love, you're not quite sure you're ready to make a pivotal life decision at this point in your life, just one year out of college. Eddie has at least four more years of this sea turtle study left before he can consider relocating (and he's not itching to move either, and certainly not to the States).

At the same time, the idea of returning to the US to begin adulting sounds downright claustrophobic, especially after the freedom you've experienced here. You do still feel a desire to both prove yourself and make the world a little better; however, your conviction for the former and your belief in the latter as being attainable from within "the system" have both diminished from a year ago.

You feel like you're going to be hit with heartbreak either way you turn. But, alas, you have to act, one way or the other.

If you decide to stay in Costa Rica indefinitely, get a teaching job, and shack up with Eddie, turn to Chapter 5.

If you decide to stay in touch with Eddie but return to the States to follow through with your intention to dive into your career after a year abroad, turn to Chapter 3.

3

TRANSITION BACK

You leave Costa Rica with a broken heart. Although you believe that returning to the States—and to your planned career journey—is the right decision long-term, it hurts like hell right now.

With no place to live and no job lined up yet, you very-temporarily move back in with your mother while you get your bearings. Fortunately, she makes it very easy for you to keep that goal of brevity. As you lie in bed crying and listening to Spanish love songs, your mother gives you enough concerned check-ins to get you off your ass and looking ahead.

You email, call, and text with Eddie. As you do, a surprising revelation starts to emerge: once you take away the tropical backdrop, and when you're not staring into his deep, mesmerizing eyes, or making out in the sweet humidity of the rainforest, you don't actually have as much to talk about as you remembered. It's only a few weeks before your sorrow turns into neutrality, followed by a tinge of relief.

You dust off your old resume, add a few lines about the life experience you gained from your year in Central America, and start sending it out.

You slowly move on, and as you do, you go to Chapter 4.

4

PASSION OR PROSPERITY

You knew your first "real" job wouldn't just fall in your lap, but you didn't quite expect just how far from your lap it would be. You've spent months and increasingly sleepless nights sending out resumes, having networking coffees with third-degree connections like your father's college roommate's wife, and LinkedIn stalking what feels like anyone with a manager title. And you've gone from a search criterion of "a socially impactful role focused on analyzing and communicating big data at a culture-driven, innovative company" to "any job that pays more than minimum wage and requires some level of thinking and communicating."

You've moved in with a new roommate, Macy, who is getting a PhD in environmental science. She's barely around, and when she is, she's locked in her room with her painfully philosophical boyfriend. You've been paying your share of the rent by bartending at a college pub in the evenings (you can't seem to get away from these college kids!) while doing your job search by day. It's all you can do to shower the bar stink out of your hair before collapsing into bed at 2:30 A.M.

Then one morning, you awake to an alert about an email from your high school English teacher's cousin (seriously . . . you've been networking with *everyone*!). It turns out, her friend is hiring a content editor for the website of a large bank. Although it's not what you pictured as your dream job, it does sound way healthier—and more in line with your communications degree—than pouring drinks with names like "blue balls" and "rockstar blaster" for frat boys. You apply immediately.

Three weeks and two phone calls later, you find yourself in an awkwardly fitting second-hand Ann Taylor suit explaining to a hiring manager named Pete why you are passionate about financial institutions as a means toward human empowerment. You think to yourself how ridiculous that sounds as you're saying it, but Pete seems to be eating it up. He says he'll get back to you in the coming days.

That evening you go out with a few friends to the local Taco Tuesday happy hour and recap your interview. You are going on about how excited you are to pour yourself into a job that you love, and how difficult it is to find meaningful employment that is actually . . . meaningful, when a woman at the next table turns to you.

"Sorry for eavesdropping. I'm actually hiring an office manager—I can let you know how to apply if you are interested." It turns out the woman, Stacey Allen, is the executive director of a nonprofit that trains Seeing Eye dogs. That sounds much more meaningful to you, and you exchange contact info with Stacey, promising to follow up in the morning.

You go through a series of interviews with Stacey and her leadership team. You also hear back from Pete. Somehow, the unthinkable has happened: you have gone from zero job prospects to two job offers in the course of three weeks. And you don't know what to do.

On the one hand, the bank job is more related to your degree, has plenty of opportunity for advancement, and pays 43 percent more than the nonprofit.

On the other hand, you—like 62 percent of your generation—feel more inclined to work for a company that is doing good than one where you can make loads of money.[1] Seeing Eye dogs are awesome because they're dogs (you love dogs, and still desperately miss your childhood labradoodle, Coco), and The Seeing Eye is a well-established, proven institution that makes a real contribution to the lives of people who are vision impaired. That's compelling.

You spend the rest of the week deliberating. To your surprise, this choice is actually more upsetting than liberating. It feels heavy in its significance. You make lists of pros and cons, assign weightings to each factor, and try to calculate the right decision. But math can't save you this time, and you need to make the call.

If you decide to go with the less-risky, more lucrative bank role, since it is more in line with your education, go to **Chapter 7**.

If you decide to go with the more impactful role at The Seeing Eye nonprofit, go to **Chapter 6**.

5

HAPPILY EVER AFTER
IN THE RAINFOREST

You start your day the way you start every day: you roll over, give Eddie a kiss, and then slip out of bed while he's still drifting. You feed the two street dogs that have become accustomed to food at your door (you've given them the names Lady and Tramp, although you suspect they're both tramps) and make yourself a breakfast of mango, yogurt, and coffee.

Then you head off to the zip-lining adventure park where you've become an eco-tourism guide—a fancy title for strapping tourists into harnesses and giving them a safety speech... forty times a day. But it pays the bills and lets you stay in Costa Rica, a place that you are learning to love and respect, and it gives you time to explore the first relationship that has swept you away.

This lifestyle fills you with deep excitement and pleasure for about the first six months. Then general contentment for another nine to twelve. And then the repetition of work, along with the emerging realization that the life Eddie imagines for himself and the expectations you have of yourself may ultimately be prohibitively incompatible. You realize that Eddie's academic career ambitions, their lack of flexibility, and the fact that your life and dreams would always come second to his just will not make you happy.

Although you have started to feel that being with Eddie long-term isn't the way you see yourself living the rest of your days (since you're only twenty-five, and hopefully have many, many more days), and eco-tourism isn't exactly your dream job either, you don't regret staying in Central America. The people, the language, the climate, the food—you have grown to love and respect them, and you are not ready to leave just yet.

And so you move on from the parts that aren't meant to be—namely your boyfriend and your job. With the goal of writing a book cataloging tropical plants, you travel to a town in Ecuador where some friends you made previously moved.

While you are writing this book, you meet a new man: Antonio. He is also a writer, covering Ecuadorian politics in the local newspaper. You are reserved for a while, but you become friends, and eventually fall madly in love in a way that you haven't known before.

Antonio has a sister named Paula who is your age, and the two of you become close as well. She brings you into her fold of friends, and before long, you feel the kind of sisterhood that you haven't felt since you were in the college dorms.

You and Antonio settle down and spend the rest of your days writing, traveling and, eventually, raising three babies in the rainforest of Ecuador. It is nothing that you ever expected, but it is perfect for you now.

The End

(Want to see what would have happened if you returned to the States instead? Turn back to Chapter 2 and make a different choice. Or if you've explored all the paths, turn to the Epilogue.)

6

REEDUCATE OR REPRIORITIZE

You put down the phone and jump up to move an enormous box full of dog harnesses out of the hallway and into the break room. As you come back to your desk, a new group of volunteers walks in, ready for their training, but the volunteer coordinator is also the fund development director, and she is on an important call about the upcoming luncheon. So you take the volunteers into the training room (which doubles as the accounting office) and start introducing them to the history of the organization. Just then, a big shipment of dog food comes in, so you have to run out to sign for it, at which point the phone starts ringing again.

This is your life, Monday through Friday from 8:30 A.M. to 5:00 P.M. You had no idea that the title office manager would actually translate to person-who-does-everything-because-we're-permanently-short-staffed. Although it's frantic and scattered and exhausting, you do kind of love it. The dogs that your organization raises and trains absolutely melt your heart, the people you get to work with are some of the kindest and smartest you've met, and the clients who end up with the dogs gain access to a level of freedom and self-determination they never thought they would have—all of which is deeply rewarding.

Unfortunately, you're barely scraping by with your nonprofit salary. You've had to keep a couple of bartending shifts in the evenings in order to make ends meet, and even so, you're consuming an unhealthy amount of ramen and Cheerios. This level of time commitment between two jobs, and the exhaustion from the pace of them, means that you don't have much of a life right now.

Stacey, the executive director, has become a mentor to you. In her, you see the level of expertise, success, and work-life balance that you aspire to. She has been kind enough to make time to provide you with guidance and support—a commitment you feel fortunate to have, as only 54 percent of women have access to senior leaders as mentors.[1] You confide in her that you love what you're doing, but that you don't feel that your current pace is sustainable, and also that you still feel a nagging self-doubt about not really using the skills you went to school for.

Stacey suggests that if you're serious about rising in the nonprofit ranks, you might want to consider going back to school to pursue a master's in public administration in nonprofit management. With the number of nonprofit employees growing at record rates, competition for leadership roles is steep.[2] You would love to be able to move up in your career while doing good in the world. Although another two years of school and more student debt doesn't sound entirely awesome to you, which is perhaps why only about 4.5 percent of your generation is enrolled in graduate programs each year, you believe that you'd be able to pay back the additional loans once you make it into a nonprofit leadership role.[3]

Your good friend Mara went the corporate track, and while you've been breaking your back with multitasking, she has already gotten a promotion, is able to eat out at restaurants—a simple yet coveted activity—and has found time to start throwing pottery. You act a little self-righteous in the nobility of your chosen career path, but if you're honest with yourself, you're a little envious. Which is why, when Mara tells you that a role just opened on her team for a content editor, you wonder if it would hurt to just apply and see.

The one thing you know for sure is you need to make some kind of change, for sanity's sake.

If you decide to go back to school for your master's in public administration in order to go after aspirations of nonprofit leadership even though it would put you further in debt, go to Chapter 9.

If you decide to apply for the content editor role at Mara's company and find ways to change the world in your spare time, go to Chapter 7.

7

FOLLOW YOUR HEART
OR YOUR IDEALS

You sit in your cubical, staring at your computer screen, trying to give yourself a mental therapy session before the status meeting in nine minutes. The unsettling combination of almost constantly feeling overqualified and underqualified in your job is giving you a complex that you've never experienced before.

You feel overqualified because this work is actually pretty easy. You're given placeholder text for different content on the bank website and apps, and you edit that text to sound articulate and in line with the company's brand. On occasion, you even get to write a little blurb to explain a concept, like savings account interest or overdraft fees. It's not exactly rocket science, and you're doing fine at it. Your manager seems to like you, and you've made a few friends with whom you enjoy eating lunch and critiquing the soft drink selection, as well as the wardrobe choices of a few more interestingly dressed executives.

At the same time, you feel underqualified. You often find yourself sitting in meetings and feeling embarrassed for even being there because you don't know what value you bring to the table. Everyone around you appears to be brilliant, as they banter, throw big ideas out there, and reference case studies and experiences that you have no awareness of. This feeling of being out of place—as though you accidentally walked into a planning meeting for an aircraft carrier instead of the weekly user experience review—is only exacerbated by the fact that when you do try to pipe up and say something, no one usually seems to notice. Someone with a louder voice will start talking as though your quiet words were actually only in your head after all. Or if you do get them out, the next comment will not be in response to yours, but on a different thought altogether. And then, on occasion, someone else says the same thing you just did, and everyone wholeheartedly agrees with them. It makes you feel invisible.

You learn later in life that what you are experiencing now is an example of a painful but extremely common condition called *imposter syndrome* –a feeling of psychological discomfort brought on by difficulty acknowledging one's own success, which an estimated 70 percent of the US population has experienced at some point.[1] You are also being subjected to *microaggressions*—the subtle forms of discriminatory behavior that 64 percent of women experience at work, with much higher rates for women of color and lesbian women.[2] But for now, you just feel like the parts of your job that you find easy are probably due to you not understanding their complexity and that you are on the verge of being exposed as a fraud.

Outside of work you're also battling other complexes of the dating variety. You've been meeting a variety of young men through a combination of Tinder, Bumble, and introductions from friends. Although some of the dates are fun, and more of them result in humorous stories, you're finding that just the act of putting yourself out there is almost a second full-time job. Previously, you met boyfriends though school or groups of friends, and the relationships formed organically. This goal-based dating is exhausting.

That state of exhaustion is where you are residing when the final straw—or, specifically, the final unsolicited dick pic—prompts you to shut down your online dating accounts. You decide to write off dating for a while, which of course, by the laws of the universe, means that three days later, while running an emergency toothpaste, peanut butter, and wine grocery store trip in your pajama bottoms and your old high school volleyball t-shirt, you meet Nathan in the checkout line.

You smile at each other. You see a twinkle in his blue-gray eyes. You remember what you're wearing and blush. "Oh, you like your peanut butter crunchy too. Cool!" he says. And that's all it takes.

You and Nathan start hanging out. A lot. You have an awesome combination of chemistry and compatibility—dynamics that you can only ever remember feeling one of strongly at a time in past relationships. And your friends love him too, which is a high bar to achieve!

As time progresses, you find yourself in a state that feels both familiar, in the regularity of the activities and relationships that surround you, and also unfamiliar in that you've never felt quite so calm and happy before. Although you still experience some anxieties and restlessness at work, and of course you and Nathan have the occasional disagreements (ok, yelling matches), you have settled into a state of general comfort. You've gotten promoted to senior content specialist, you've met Nathan's parents (and they're quite lovely) and he has met yours, and you have a third Sunday dinner party with a group of close friends. This adulting isn't bad.

That is, until Nathan gets an offer for his dream job—across the country. He has been working as a marketing manager for an online shoe store, which he's enjoyed, but has been feeling limited career growth as of late. A sporting goods retailer in Portland, Oregon, reached out to him and offered him a director of marketing role, and he is through the roof about it. You want to be happy for him, but this throws your life into a tailspin.

Although you and Nathan haven't been living together yet, you have been discussing the idea. And you have definitely been discussing your feelings for each other: you are very much in love. He asks you if you would be willing to move to Portland and move in together there. It makes you happy that he'd like you to move with him but sad that he seems to have already made up his mind about moving regardless of your answer.

You've been to Portland once, for a friend's wedding (she doesn't live there anymore, though), and it seemed like a great city. However, you like where you're living now too, and you mostly like your job. You wouldn't be considering moving if it weren't for Nathan. The feminist in you is cringing at the idea of uprooting your life and making a decision purely based on the job prospects of your boyfriend . . . you always saw yourself as someone who would only make major life decisions for your own reasons.

You go out with your friend Mara and your aunt Ashley for a sip-and-paint night and ask for their advice. Mara feels strongly that you shouldn't move just for a boy, although you suspect this might be slightly influenced by her not wanting you to leave—a sentiment that you feel too. Ashley, however, surprises you by telling you about the "one who got away"—a former boyfriend who you don't even remember, but who apparently broke her heart when you were only in junior high. Both Mara and Ashley are strong women whom you love and respect, and you feel like right now they are playing the role of angel and devil on your shoulders. Although you're not sure who is who.

If you decide to quit your job, pack up your apartment, and move to a brand-new city with Nathan, go to Chapter 8.

If you decide to try keeping in touch with Nathan long-distance but aren't ready to leave your whole life behind for a man, go to Chapter 10.

8

REPORT OR RECOIL

You and Nathan are living in a cute mid-century duplex in Portland's Pearl District. It took a good six months to start to feel at home here, and there were times when you felt far from it, but you're pleasantly surprised by how natural it feels to wake up every day next to Nathan, to walk to the corner coffee shop for a soy Americano and morning glory muffin, and to sit reading the *New Yorker* together on a Sunday morning. It's cute.

Now that you're settled in, you don't feel like you compromised yourself by following a man across the country. After all, it wasn't just any man: you two are deeply in love. And besides, you're still the same you over here in Portland and not any less of a feminist. You even found a job that's similar to your last one, with slightly better benefits, and have been ramping up nicely in your new role.

Your new job is at a consulting firm that provides project management, content, and marketing services to medium-to-large tech companies. You're doing similar copy-editing work to your last job but also get the chance to manage some of the projects, which you enjoy. Your manager, Robert, seems really nice, and he encourages you to go after your goals.

One day you and Robert go to meet with a potential client, who turns out to be a little rude. Not egregiously so, but he talks down to you in a noticeable enough way that after the meeting, Robert asks if you want to grab a drink to shake it off. "I'm so sorry he treated you like that . . . that was bullshit," he tells you. You appreciate Robert's concern and say yes to the drink.

You two belly-up at the bar at Red Robin, in between some after-work nurses in scrubs and what looks like an awkward first or second date. Robert talks about the worst client meetings he's ever had, and you both laugh at the ridiculous stories.

You're on your second glass of hefeweizen when Robert leans over and rubs your shoulder in a . . . friendly way? You feel weird about this and try to subtly scoot back, which gets him to move his hand. But then he rests it casually on your thigh. Shit, you think, did you bring this on yourself by agreeing to have drinks with him? Or maybe he didn't mean to put his hand there? No, that wouldn't make sense. You wait for 30 seconds so that you don't seem like you're reacting dramatically and then say that you need to get back to the office to finish up a few things.

That night, you feel awful—and even more confusingly, you can only describe it as feeling somehow dirty. You don't mention the incident to Nathan because you feel like you shouldn't have said yes to drinks and because you don't want him freaked out about you going to work. Besides, you've got this handled . . . you'll just make sure you're never in a situation like that with Robert again.

That plan works. For a while. A few weeks later, you drop off an edited document with Robert. As you're leaving, he says, "I love how you wear those jeans so that I'll stare at your ass. It totally works." You can feel your face turn bright red, and your best reaction is to pretend not to have heard him and just keep walking.

Again, you start to doubt yourself: are your jeans too tight? Do you give off the wrong vibe? You feel mortified.

Two nights later, Robert texts you at 10:15 P.M., just as you and Nathan are watching your final episode of *West Wing*. "Can't stop thinking about u. It's making me hard. Why do u do this to me?"

You finally realize you can't avoid the situation anymore. You start to cry and tell Nathan what's been going on. He's sad that you didn't feel comfortable telling him sooner, but he understands. He's livid with Robert (who he's only met once) and is ready to show up at his house and punch him in the face.

You convince Nathan that the face punch isn't the smartest move, and you two stay up talking about options. You decide the right thing to do—even though it's scary—is to go to your head of HR and let her know what Robert has been doing. You finally drift off to sleep around 1:00 A.M., with a plan and your resolve.

Two days later, you show up to your meeting with Lindsay in HR. You painstakingly tell her the details of how Robert has been harassing you and even tear up a couple times. And so you are shocked when she looks you in the eye, smiles a sympathetic smile, and tells you that that's just Robert, always testing boundaries. She goes on to say that Robert is one of the company's top managers, and you should feel flattered that he likes you. "Just don't egg him on and this will all blow over," she says. "He'll move his attention on to someone else soon enough."

You're completely in shock. You feel like all the air has been pushed out of your lungs, but you manage to say something vaguely coherent as you leave the HR director's office in a daze. Of all of the hypothetical outcomes that were swirling through your head, this one never occurred to you. Unfortunately, had you looked at the stats, you might have expected this . . . only an estimated 6 to 13 percent of people harassed at work actually report it, and of those who do, 75 percent face retaliation.[1] You and Nathan go back to the drawing board.

It seems like you need to either quit and find a new job or out Robert publicly. Quitting definitely seems like the easier choice, and one that would protect you from reputation-related consequences. But you can't help but think about what Lindsay said about Robert moving on to someone else. How many women has he done this to before, and how many are still to come?

Just as you're pondering this, you get a text from Robert. "I just came thinking about that sweater you were wearing today. You're such a tease."

You have to act.

If you decide to quietly quit your job, not draw attention to yourself while you're still early in your career, and find a new job elsewhere, turn to Chapter 14.

If you decide to take a stand for all womankind and report Robert's behavior—and the company's reaction—to the local business journal, go to Chapter 12.

9

LOVE OR MARRIAGE

You are halfway through your master's program and are really enjoying it. Although you don't love the accumulating debt—especially while many of your friends are progressing further in their careers—you are learning a lot and making some really cool new friends.

You've started dating a guy named Silas from your Organizational Leadership class. He's a little aloof, but he makes you laugh and he's extremely sexy. You and Silas spend many evenings in his apartment, studying, debating, and having amazing sex. It's not a bad lifestyle.

You had to quit your office manager job at the Seeing Eye nonprofit in order to go back to school full time. Although Stacey said she'd find a role for you there when you graduate, and you told her (sincerely) that you would love to come back, your coursework focusing on social innovation has you thinking even bigger now. You want to reimagine entire community structures and social systems.

You attend a weekend social impact hackathon in partnership with the college of engineering that focuses on using technology to address homelessness. You are so moved and invigorated by the possibilities that emerge from this process that you want to pursue this direction further in your studies. Unfortunately, the morning your hackathon team is going to present your project, you feel sick and need to run home. But the seed has been planted for you, and you're excited to take a Technology in Social Work course next semester to further explore this path.

To your shock, it turns out that your interest in technology as a means toward social impact wasn't the only seed that was planted. After a couple of weeks of that "sickness" you were feeling, you take a pregnancy test. Holy shit: you're pregnant! You're 96 percent sure that you and Silas have been using condoms every single time. And they're 98 percent effective. And there's only a 15 percent chance of getting pregnant in a given month even if you *were* trying.[1] So you calculate that the odds of this happening were about one in ten thousand— another time when your math proves to be irrelevant.

You tell your close friend Anna before you even think of telling Silas. At first you share the news with her in a calm, stunned state. But as you start to say out loud what you hadn't allowed yourself to think—that you're not sure you are ready to keep this baby—you start to cry uncontrollable sobs for the first time since you found out. For Anna, this brings up the time she had an abortion in college, as 24 percent of women in the US do before age 45.[2] Before you know it, you are both sitting on your couch, crying buckets into the bowl of cheesy popcorn that sits between you.

By the end of the conversation, you feel as if you have some clarity: even though the timing isn't what you would have chosen by a long shot, you have always felt that you wanted to be a mother someday. And it's unexpected how much you feel yourself connecting with this lentil-sized creature that is somehow already making your jeans too tight.

That's not to say that you're not terrified—you are. You don't know how you'll finish your degree, how you'll support this baby, or how you'll become enough of a grownup in eight months to be someone's parent. But you've made up your mind, so you'll just have to figure it out. You and Anna embrace, and you steady yourself to share the news with Silas.

• • •

Silas is surprisingly excited. At first, he looked like he was about to pass out and said that he needed some time to process the news. But within a few days, his panic is replaced with unexpected enthusiasm. A few weeks after that, it's replaced with something even more surprising.

You and Silas are eating spaghetti in his apartment—one of the only foods that doesn't make your stomach churn these days—when he almost casually says to you, "I've been thinking. We should get married." There goes the spaghetti.

Once you get back from puking your dinner out, you tell Silas you're blown away and need to think about it.

Silas is a good guy, and the chemistry is definitely there (or at least it was before your internal chemistry got hijacked). The fact that he's excited about this baby and *wants* to marry you says a lot about his character. But when you dig deep, the physical chemistry and shared interests are really all that has held you together. You have never connected with him on a deeper level than that, and you're not sure you ever will. Maybe you're being too idealistic, but you always thought the man you married would be someone who moved you down to your soul.

You know that it would certainly be easier to raise a child with a father than as a single mother, although children with single mothers do make up 23 percent of family arrangements, so you wouldn't be alone going that route.[3] And who knows . . . maybe you could grow to feel a deeper connection with him over time.

Silas is keeping his distance, waiting for an answer from you. You know that you need to make a decision . . . if only to avoid having the potential marriage look like a shotgun wedding if you do decide to marry him.

If you choose to say yes to Silas and marry for practicality over true love, go to Chapter 11.

If you decide to hold on to your ideals of marrying for love and give Silas the option of sticking around to co-parent, go to Chapter 13.

10

LEAN IN OR ACROSS

You hang up the phone after another one of your two-hour conversations and drift off to sleep. You and Nathan have been talking every night for hours—a habit that is both lovely in its emotional intimacy and excruciating in its lack of physical intimacy. Having these evening debriefs has made you observe the mundane details of life with new humor and appreciation, as though you are in a constant state of preparing an interesting story to tell about your day. And because Nathan is the reason for this new state of mindfulness, you can't help but feel an ever-growing feeling of affection and longing for him.

Another shift, since Nathan has been across the country and you have few distractions other than those nighttime phone calls, is that you have plunged headfirst into your work. You may be trying to prove to yourself that staying put has meaning, but regardless of your reasoning, your manager has noticed. In one of your one-on-one meetings with her, she tells you that the company has decided to create a mobile app that provides content and calculators to help people plan their finances, and that you are being considered to lead the small team that will be working on it. You are excited!

That evening you tell Nathan the good news. And you're a little taken aback by his apparent lack of enthusiasm. After a bit of prying, he confesses that he had still been hoping you would change your mind and move to be with him, and that this promotion would make that possibility even less likely. Upon consideration, you have to admit that this is true.

You also know that moving into this management role would mean really leaning into your work . . . you don't see any mid-level managers at your company who appear to have any semblance of a work/life balance. Your good friend Mara is one of them, since she was promoted into people management six months ago. You see less of her now, and upon questioning, she admits that she's feeling spread pretty thin. But she's also really enjoying her career growth and encourages you to seize the opportunity.

Part of you thinks that if you're going to have a period in your life where you go all-in to your career, you might as well do it now before you have more attachments and obligations (like the family you've always wanted to start). But another part of you is already feeling a little lonely and isolated, and you worry that building your life around your career will just exasperate that.

Nathan comes back for a visit, and you two spend a long weekend together, barely leaving your bedroom. The feel of him reminds you of what you've been missing and makes the thought of him leaving unbearable. He must be thinking the same thing, because he turns to you with tears in his eyes on Sunday evening, before his early-morning flight the next day. "I love you so much, and I just can't keep putting myself through this indefinitely," he confides.

Nathan goes on to tell you that if you take that promotion and don't feel up to moving, he thinks you two should end things. This long-distance longing is too painful, and he wants to make a life with someone. Preferably you. This sounds like an ultimatum, and at first you get angry. But after talking it through, you understand where he is coming from, and you feel it too.

The next week, the decision becomes real: you do get offered the promotion.

As though you've been given a second chance, you once again have the choice between a relationship and work—but this time with higher stakes. Going with work means leaning in and putting your personal life on hold. Going with Nathan means finally making that big cross-country move and leaning out from work a bit as you find a new job and start over with proving yourself.

If you decide to take the promotion, focus on your career, and end things for good with Nathan, go to Chapter 15.

If you decide to turn down the promotion and move to Portland to shack up with Nathan, go to Chapter 8.

11

RENT OR BUY

Despite wanting to avoid the appearance of a shotgun wedding, your wedding dress has had to be expanded a few times in recent weeks. But your bump is super cute, and you actually love the way the off-white lace falls over it.

The weeks leading up to your wedding have been a confusing fluctuation of emotions. Sadness, excitement, fear, and happiness. Rinse and repeat. Between the hormonal roller coaster that comes with growing a human in your body, the mild stress of pursuing a challenging graduate degree, and the mixed feelings you have about planning a circumstance-driven wedding, you don't even know what version of your emotions you'll be met with when you open your eyes each morning.

Even though the circumstances leading up to your wedding were fairly off-script from your youthful fantasies, the wedding itself turns out to be lovely. And not nearly as stressful as Hollywood might have had you believe. You have an intimate ceremony and celebration, with about fifty of your and Silas's family and close friends. You didn't even meet his parents until after you said yes to his unceremonious proposal, so you feel fortunate that you didn't inadvertently stumble into a crazy in-law situation. They're a little more conservative and meddling than your own family, but they are extremely excited about their impending grandchild and seem fond of you already.

Your parents have been slightly less joyous over the thought of becoming grandparents already. They've been predictably supportive of you, but neither of them has a great poker face, and you can see the concern and residual shock in their eyes. You're well past the window of teen pregnancy at the ripe old age of twenty-six. But your parents—like you—had assumed you would be out of grad school, gainfully employed, and intentionally partnered up before you started spawning. It's just taking them a little time to get used to the situation.

You would think that the new marriage, motherhood, and the last year of your master's would be the most overwhelming things on your mind. But the change that is looming most dauntingly for you—perhaps because it's the only one that's not already decided on—is where you and Silas will live. Up to this point, you were focused on all of the aforementioned changes and have been keeping your own living arrangements until you got past the wedding. Your roommate has already lined up a new tenant to move in next month, and Silas's one-bedroom apartment will be too cramped for a new family of three, so the time has come for you to find somewhere to live together.

Your home search is complicated right out of the gate since you are both current students and don't have a great proof of income other than student loan documents. But Silas's parents generously offer to cosign for you. Even though you're both in school right now, it's a pretty safe bet to assume you'll both be working near downtown once you graduate . . . assuming you don't decide to move to a different city.

Although the unknown of where you'll be working coupled with your current lack of income makes you think that renting a place downtown would be prudent, there's a new nesting side of you that can't stop fantasizing about buying a home in which to really settle down. If you did buy, you would opt for a place outside of downtown, where your little mango-sized decision-driver would have room to play and you would have community to foster.

Silas's parents really love the idea of you settling down in the suburbs and, in addition to cosigning, are willing to help you out with a down payment. This is nice of them but it also makes you a bit uncomfortable. It already seems as if they're pushing their presence into your lives more than you prefer, and you worry that feeling indebted to them in this way will make your desire for boundaries more difficult to negotiate. You know that, financially, it only makes sense to buy a home if you plan to stay in it for several years, which will narrow your job options to local ones once you graduate.[1]

Even though, rationally, you see all of the challenges you might face as a result of accepting assistance from Silas's parents and narrowing your job search options to those surrounding you, you can't help but feel drawn toward the dream of starting a family in a home of your own. Perhaps it is because so much else around you feels fleeting and uncertain, but the thought of a nest of your own is pulling on you. Like 55 percent of your generational peers, you love the mental picture of a cute little home in the suburbs for your cute little family.[2]

Most of your friends live in the city, though, and although you know you would eventually make new friends, you've seen other friends move further away and slowly lose touch. The thought of sacrificing the morning coffees and weekend walks with some of your closest girlfriends gives you pause.

If you decide to accept a down payment from Silas's parents, commit to living in the same place for at least the next five years, and look to buy a home in the suburbs, go to Chapter 16.

If you decide that you want to avoid the reliance on Silas's somewhat-overbearing parents, keep your options more open for relocation, and find an apartment rental in the city near your friends, go to Chapter 18.

12

PUNCH IT OUT

You check your email and see fifty-two new messages. And it's only been an hour since you last checked. After a cursory scan, you see that roughly five of them are from news outlets looking for interviews and quotes. Fifteen of them are from new and old friends sending loving thoughts. Thirteen are from strangers offering their support, and twelve are from strangers calling you a whore. The rest is just spam . . . which is actually a welcome inbox filler for the first time ever.

What happened to you certainly wasn't unique—a reported 38 percent of women have experienced sexual harassment in the workplace.[1] But the timing of your report happened to be opportune (or inopportune, as the case may be), in that a reporter at the local paper was working on a story about workplace harassment. She asked you if she could name you and cite your story, and after much deliberation, you agreed.

Since then, your life has taken on a very new cadence. Everyone wants to hear from you, and everyone seems to have an opinion on what went down and what role you played in it. One positive thing that comes from all of the publicity is that Sam, your college best friend, reaches out to get back in touch.

With all of the varied reactions from acquaintances, it feels comforting to hear from someone who really knows you. The two of you FaceTime for over an hour catching up, and she shares that she went through something similar in her first job. She took the leave silently route and says she admires your courage. You tell her how much her reaching out and sharing has meant to you, and the two of you promise not to lose touch again.

You've never been a person who loved being the center of attention, so this three-ring circus has had you near your breaking point on several occasions. But the support you have received from both friends and strangers, and the stories that other women have shared with you about their own workplace harassment traumas, has kept you from slipping over.

One woman from Nebraska wrote and said that your story gave her the courage to come forward about a coworker who had been sending her nasty emails for over a year . . . and that her HR department handled the situation appropriately and fired him. Another woman told you that your story validated her own history of workplace harassment, which she had been lying to herself about for ages. These stories have given you the strength to keep going through this soul-crushing time.

Nathan has given you so much strength too. He has been by your side unwaveringly throughout this. You can see in his eyes how painful it is to watch this all go down, but he is proving himself to be strong enough to handle it.

With Nathan's support, you decide to stay out of work until the news cycle blows over. You feel too self-conscious applying for jobs while this is going on, and you could use the time for self-care. During this break, you drop in on a kickboxing class at your gym one day. You end up loving it—the exercise makes you feel healthier, and the punching and kicking makes you feel strong and empowered. This makes sense, as self-defense has long been taught as a supplement to therapy for harassment victims.[2] You start taking kickboxing every morning, you feel in the best shape of your life, and learning how to take physical agency over yourself is helping you combat the helplessness and feelings of violation that you are still fighting and processing after Robert's harassment.

It is in this new healing and fit state that you continue on to Chapter 14.

13

NATURAL OR MEDICATED

You are lying in the bedroom of your new one-bedroom apartment—just you and the dynamic watermelon in your belly. When you told Silas that you didn't want to marry him just because you're pregnant and that you weren't sure you loved him in that way, he got really upset and hasn't returned any of your calls and texts since. You deduce that this means he is out of the picture. Although it's mildly terrifying to step into single motherhood with your eyes wide open (and your resume quite short), the fact that you haven't felt overly sad about Silas's absence has been a good validation of your decision.

You've moved into your own apartment since your roommate wasn't exactly looking for a loud and stinky third tenant. It's actually really nice having your own place for the first time in your life. That's not to say that you don't end up lying in bed crying at least twice a week out of a combination of fear for the future, lack of control over the present, and throbbing hips. But you have a cute bassinet set up next to your full-sized bed, a couch that your dad was getting rid of that reminds you of your own childhood, and the same Ikea desk you had in college, which provides you with a familiar spot to study. It's home.

You are thirty-nine weeks and two days pregnant, and as you lie there feeling your baby kick, you are filled with both a calm contentment and an insatiable urge to meet this little creature. You didn't find out the gender, so you just keep referring to the baby as whatever fruit or vegetable your pregnancy book tells you it is this week.

You have been going to baby classes, accompanied by your good friend Anna, and feel a little sad and self-conscious among all the happy couples, but not overly so. As Anna holds you in your squatting positions and practices funny breathing patterns with you, you feel an intimacy of friendship that you don't remember ever having in your romantic relationships. In these classes, you learn how to swaddle the baby, how to breastfeed, what kinds of poop to look out for, and what positions might be helpful during labor. You also get some help with writing out your birth plan: the ideal course of events that you hope your birth will follow.

In your birth plan, you have stated that you hope to have a natural childbirth, without any pain medications. This plan scares you a bit—in addition to the scary birth narrative you learned from Hollywood, a couple of friends who already have children have recounted their stories, and your aunt Ashley, who has two kids, swears by the epidural. But you've also heard that it's better for the baby not to have those drugs in your system and that your own recovery will be faster without them. You've even heard that women who have labor induced with an epidural are six times more likely to end up with a C-section.[1] So you brave ahead with your plan, visualizing flowers opening and waves undulating and reciting mantras about trusting your body.

As you're lying in bed this particular evening, the familiar discomfort is replaced with some pretty painful cramping. Then even more painful cramping. It takes you a few cycles to realize that these are the early-stage contractions that you've been thinking about for months! You call your doctor, who tells you to come down when they are four minutes apart, and then you phone Anna to take you to the hospital. She's offered to be your on-call buddy until your mom is able to make the drive there, which will take a couple of hours.

As your labor progresses, and your consciousness of your surroundings is replaced with a singular awareness of your own body, you learn quickly what this labor pain is all about. After about seven hours, you are sitting on a yoga ball in a shower—where did this ball or this shower even come from?— and you realize that somehow someone must have let a cage of lions into the hospital and they are now eating through your abdomen by way of your asshole. Which is to say, you might be ready to consider that epidural.

Although you feel like the last person in the world who should be making a conscious decision right now, you are, in fact, the one who needs to make it. Do you want to keep going through this excruciating, exhausting, mind-bending pain—as you had planned—and risk being too late to get an epidural later? Or do you want to scrap your natural birth plan—like 30 percent of women who end up getting an epidural do—and get some immediate relief?[2]

If you choose to stick out the pain and hope the lions don't eat you alive, go to Chapter 17.

If you choose to get an epidural and risk the regret of not being able to see your plan through, along with a cascade of potential complications, go to Chapter 19.

14

CREATE CHILDREN OR ADVENTURES

Finding a new job wasn't too difficult. And the silver lining to the whole heinous Robert situation is that you actually much prefer this new company to where you were. That disgusting maggot turned out to be just the forcing function you needed to find a better role. You are now working for a green energy company writing their marketing materials. You feel good about the indirect impact your work will have on the environment, and you really like your new team.

Making it through such a gut-wrenching time in your last job brought you and Nathan even closer together. You learned that you can trust him, and his tenderness toward you has grown deeper. So much so that, after the dust associated with recovering from your trauma and ramping up on your new job has settled, he has asked you to marry him. This doesn't even feel like a decision—he is the one for you.

Neither of you wants a big ceremony, and you're across the country from your family, so you decide to get dressed up in the gaudiest thrift store vintage ensembles you can find and hit the courthouse with a couple of your friends as witnesses. You laugh the whole time, take a few selfies, and then go out for a ridiculous celebration dinner at a hole-in-the-wall Thai restaurant. You both know that you'll have to go through the motions of a big family wedding celebration back East, but right now this is just for the two of you. And you just saved about $31,000 off the average cost of a wedding.[1] It feels like the perfect day.

. . .

Three months later you are on the edge of a cliff-top monastery outside of Barcelona, staring at the vast rocky valley beneath you. You and Nathan are on your slightly belated honeymoon (you had to wait to accumulate enough vacation time at your new job), and you are having a spectacular time—sleeping late, taking siestas, eating, drinking, and dancing into all hours of the night.

You look over at Nathan with love in your eyes. Then you look just past him and see a mother wearing her baby, making kissy faces at her little cherub. You're hit with a pang of longing all of a sudden and say out loud to Nathan, "I would love to have a baby," without even processing what you're saying. You surprise yourself with the severity of that longing, where it previously wasn't much more than a distant goal. To your shock, Nathan says, "I would too." You stare at each other for a minute, smile almost bashfully, and then table the conversation for the moment.

You and Nathan have, of course, discussed offspring before, but it was always more in the abstract. You both—like 80 percent of men and 70 percent of women—have always wanted to have kids someday.[2] But this is the first time that you have talked about it in the present tense. Back at your hotel, you end up talking more about the idea. And as you do, you feel a sense of excitement.

On the one hand, this vacation is amazing, and it has you wanting more travels and adventures. Having offspring would put a damper on that for a while . . . it is not that you couldn't travel, but you wouldn't be able to have as much spontaneity and ease as you currently enjoy, and financially, it would require tradeoffs. Also, you've only been married for a few months (although you've been together for several years now). What's the hurry? And your work on environmental issues has you second-guessing if it's even the right thing to do to bring a baby into this world, since having a child can create an average of 58.6 tons of CO_2-equivalent emissions per year—not to mention the probable state of the world in the future, given its current direction.[3]

But still, now that you're allowing your brain—or maybe heart—to think about babies, you can't stop the thoughts. You're almost thirty, so it's not a bad time to start a family. Plus, you know from a few friends that the time you start trying isn't necessarily indicative of when you actually get pregnant.

Nathan looks at you, over the flickering of the fireplace in your vacation rental apartment overlooking Las Ramblas. Down below, you see people who are happy and in love and oozing with sexuality. You feel the vibe. Nathan says, "Should tonight be the night we skip protection and see what happens?" You went off the pill six months ago when it started messing with your moods too much, and so you've been using condoms since.

If you decide to give it a go, press pause on aspirations of carefree world travels, and start trying to conceive, go to *Chapter 20.*

If you decide that the excitement and adventure all around you are still calling your name louder than your biological clock and that you aren't even convinced it's the right thing to do to bring a child into the current state of the world, turn to *Chapter 21.*

15

LADDER OR JUNGLE GYM

Y ou are finally feeling comfortable in your own skin again. The early transition into managing people (a few of them older than you) and working in the new-for-you frontier of mobile apps brought back your imposter syndrome something fierce. But after almost two years of trial by fire, you are starting to feel legit.

The work your team has done has been widely adopted and recognized by the industry, and your company's leadership has recognized it in turn. As a result, your team has grown, you've been promoted to senior manager, and you have a promising career ahead, scaling and rising even further.

Although you love the feeling of success, you can't help but wonder if you're on the right path. You seem to be good at what you're doing, which feels like validation. You've often touted the idea that building mobile financial tools is making the world a better place by empowering people to really own their finances, but you don't fully believe it. You always dreamed of doing work that would improve lives, and you have a nagging feeling that this isn't it.

Your intense work schedule has also been keeping you from passions outside of work. You've always found solace and inspiration in writing, and lately you've barely had time for the occasional blog post. You miss this creative outlet.

Your close friend Stacia is going through a similar stage in her career, questioning her sense of purpose and whether she is fulfilled. After many evenings of discussing your respective careers at the wine bar down the street from your apartment, she talks you into doing a weekend career-counseling retreat. This sounds slightly ridiculous to you, but you also think a girl weekend with Stacia could be awesome regardless of the agenda. You finally agree.

After a weekend of meditation, skill assessments, personality quizzes, and yoga sessions (half of which you couldn't help rolling your eyes and snickering through), you actually emerge with some clarity. You want to be a journalist and shed light on the issues plaguing the world.

You talk to your mother on the phone the week you get back and tell her about your revelation. She tells you that it's so sweet that you want to do that, but that you really should be responsible about your career prospects, and just do some journalism on the side. You get a similar reaction from a few friends, who are already struggling through more morally fulfilling careers and can't fathom why you would want to walk away from your six-figure salary and the clear-cut career ladder laid out in front of you.

You're not alone in your desire, though—one of the most common reasons that women report staying in a job is that the job gives them the opportunity to make a difference.[1] And for people who do decide to change jobs, one in three of them end up changing careers entirely.[2] Additionally, while 74 percent of women start out their careers aspiring to executive leadership positions, that number decreases to 57 percent as women progress through their careers.[3] You wonder if you might be one of those women whose passions start to replace their corporate ambitions.

You know that becoming a journalist would require you to move to an industry that doesn't pay as well and require you to start over in a more entry-level role. You might even have to begin with an internship. But you've been doing a decent job of saving and, if you cut your spending back, you will have about six months of runway to get on your feet again. You'd also have a year of COBRA health insurance that you could buy into after leaving your job, which would be affordable enough to hold you over until you find a fulltime role.

Stacia has taken her career weekend revelations to heart and is taking baking classes to try to fulfill her dream of being a cake maker. Of course, she also has a pretty hefty safety net through her inheritance, so you can hardly compare your decision to hers.

Still, you're almost thirty. You believe that if you are going to make a major career change that involves a major reset, it is better to do so before you have too many more responsibilities to factor in.

If you decide to keep climbing the corporate ladder that is propped up and waiting for you, go to Chapter 22.

If you decide to climb the jungle gym instead, and start applying for roles in journalism, turn to Chapter 23.

16

BACK TO WORK OR STAY HOME

You slip downstairs while Zoe is still sleeping and put a pot of coffee on. You'll need it to get through the day after another night of feedings every two hours. She must be going through a growth spurt.

Now that Zoe is five months old, and begrudgingly taking a bottle when it's her only option, you are letting Silas's mom come by for a few hours a day to watch her so that you can stay on top of your school work. Silas will be graduating this semester, and you—because you took some time off for the early baby days—still have one more semester after that.

Zoe, named after Silas's maternal grandmother, is the most amazing human you have ever laid eyes on. Her every expression, babble, and movement fills you with awe. She also exhausts you in a way you never could have predicted from someone who can't even crawl yet.

You love the house that you and Silas (and his parents) bought. It's small, but it's on a beautiful tree-lined street, with a park four blocks away, and the neighbors that you have met so far seem great. Several of them even have young children, and you love the idea of Zoe having friends to grow up around.

• • •

What you don't love, once you start taking your classes back at the university the following semester (after a generous study-from-home accommodation your first semester postpartum) is your commute. It's forty minutes each way to school, and it will be even longer if you end up working downtown.

Silas has just finished his master's in public administration (MPA) and didn't have too difficult of a time finding a job after graduation. He is now working as an employee assistance program counselor, employed by an agency that is a contractor for several large, local corporations. He likes the work so far, and his salary is just enough to cover your basic living expenses if you get creatively frugal with your spending—a skill that you've already gotten good at.

The last two semesters of your master's program solidify your interest in using technology to solve social issues. Of course, you don't actually have the technical expertise (at all). But after one more hackathon (this one involving pumping in the bathroom) and a joint project with students studying for their master's in machine learning, you believe that you could forge a career around partnerships between technical and social service disciplines.

That career, however, would start out paying less than the cost of daycare. And Silas's mother has already started dropping hints that she can't continue watching Zoe every day. The high cost of childcare is a major factor for many, influencing the career decisions of 63 percent of parents.[1]

More than logistical issues, though, is the fact that you can feel a piece of your heart rip out every time you're away from your daughter. It just feels so unnatural. And now that she's almost a year old, she's starting to perform more little tricks all the time, and it makes you sad to miss so many firsts.

As you near graduation, the choice becomes real: do you start job hunting or plan to stay home with Zoe?

The idea of going through all this work to finally earn your master's and then end up not using it feels absurd to you. And you're deeply passionate about the work you could be doing.

But if you get the job you want and factor in your likely commute, you could be gone for ten hours a day. And you'd almost be financially worse off than if you didn't work, at least for the first couple of years, until you moved up in your career and childcare costs decrease with age. And you really hate the idea of missing so much of Zoe's early years.

This is a decision that so many mothers struggle with. Ultimately, 39 percent of mothers take time away from working to care for their children.[2] And you'd estimate that this stat is much higher for the moms in your neighborhood, based on conversations you've had on the playground. It seems like most of the mothers you've met have transitioned from educations and careers into full-time parenting, although that's likely skewed by the daytime playground crowd.

*If you choose to go after your dream job and find a way to make the finances and time management work, go to **Chapter 28**.*

*If you choose to stay home with Zoe and kick the career can down the road, go to **Chapter 25**.*

17

SNOT AND TEARS

You power through your labor for four and a half more hours, giving in to the waves of pain and trusting your body to do what it is meant to do. It is the worst pain you have ever experienced in your life, but when you look down afterward, you don't see teeth and claw marks where lions tore your flesh apart . . . you see your still-round but slightly deflating belly, and you see your precious daughter lying on your chest, staring back at you. You name her Lily. She is pure magic.

You feel a slight pang of not having her father there to share this moment with but are happy that your mother and Anna are there to witness this life-changing, heart-expanding experience.

And then there's the cheeseburger. The best fucking cheeseburger you have ever tasted in your life—even though it came from the hospital cafeteria and would probably taste mediocre at best under normal circumstances. This is your reward for making it through labor without drugs: instant gratification of the edible variety, since you don't need to wait for medication to wear off before you can eat.

• • •

Despite having the uncomplicated birth that you strived for, your recovery feels difficult. You experience painful constipation, crazy night sweats, and a lurking sense of worry. Your milk supply isn't sufficient to keep Lily satiated and so you finally have to give in and supplement with formula—a compromise that goes against your plans to exclusively breast feed. Thank goodness your mother has come to stay with you for the first few weeks to help with diaper changes, food for you, and bottles of formula for Lily when your chapped and bleeding nipples aren't enough.

Unfortunately, your mom has to get back home after a few weeks. You have several friends that have organized a meal train for you and who promise to visit you frequently. But you feel scared and alone.

Lily has reflux and seems to be crying most of the time. And your mind feels like it is playing tricks on you. You feel like a failure for not being able to make Lily comfortable, a failure for having a baby without a father in the picture (especially since you had the option of having him around), and a failure for not being able to stay on top of your coursework in your early days of motherhood. Soon you find yourself crying even more than Lily.

You are experiencing postpartum depression (PPD), a condition that affects as many as one in seven women after having a baby.[1] You start spending entire days and nights barely leaving your bed, crying snotty tears onto Lily's perfect velvety head.

A few of your friends who have been bringing you meals compare notes and decide you need help. Anna sits with you while you call your doctor to make an appointment, and then she drives you and Lily there two days later.

Your doctor diagnoses your PPD, prescribes you an antidepressant, and suggests counseling. You feel so low that you don't believe any of this will actually help, but you go along with her recommendations. You start on the antidepressants and begin seeing a counselor twice a week.

Slowly, your fog of despair begins to lift. You start going out with Lily for short walks, meeting friends for coffee, and generally looking toward the future again.

And as you do, you continue on to *Chapter 24.*

18

BALANCE OR DRIVE

You look around your life and barely recognize it from just a year ago. You have a gorgeous baby girl, Zoe, named after Silas's maternal grandmother, a master's in public administration, and a new job as a corporate social responsibility associate at a national office supply chain.

You, Silas, and Zoe are living in a two-bedroom apartment in a cute neighborhood close to downtown. It's a little cramped and very messy since neither of you has the time for housekeeping. But you're only a fifteen-minute bus ride from work, and you have an amazing French pastry shop half a block away, so you can't complain too much.

Starting your new job when Zoe was only three months old was brutal. You dropped her off at a daycare two blocks from your work, ran over at lunchtime to nurse her, and constantly felt self-conscious about the time you spent away from your desk as you pumped twice a day in addition to your nursing lunches.

Now that you're more established in your routine and Zoe is starting to eat some solids and wean off of daytime nursing, you feel a little more comfortable in your work routine.

But you still need to leave by five every day to pick her up from daycare since Silas is working across town. And when she gets sick, which is insanely frequent this first winter of daycare, you end up being the one to stay home with her. You don't know if it's just in your head or not, but you're starting to agree with 51 percent of working mothers who say that being a parent makes it harder to advance in their careers (as opposed to only 16 percent of working fathers).[1]

You look around and see colleagues who appear to be on the fast track. They work long hours, grab cocktails together after work, and get promoted almost annually. You recognize that this could be you if you wanted it enough. None of these career climbers have more potential, or even productivity, than you do. They just spend more time being seen and building relationships, while you power through your work efficiently during the day in order to get home for your "second shift."

But then you think about Zoe doing new things every day, largely without you there. She is saying some words now, stumbling around on two feet, and blowing kisses. You love your job and don't necessarily want to stay home with her all day, but you do wish you could be with her more than you get to. And you also feel societal pressure to be an involved mother, as is reported by 77 percent of adults.[2]

As it is, you're feeling like you kind of suck at everything. You're not putting in the face time to get ahead at work, you're not there for Zoe's special firsts, you and Silas barely have time to talk, let alone enjoy each other's company, and you still haven't lost all of your baby weight after over a year! You are like 66 percent of US employees who do not feel they have the work/life balance they want.[3]

You feel like you need to invest more in some aspect of your life so that you're not spread so thin.

Part of you wants to hire a nanny who could drop Zoe off in the morning and pick her up in the evening so you could lean in to your work more. This is the phase in your career where you could really start climbing like your colleagues are. And maybe it's better for you to be going all in on your work while Zoe's younger so you can be more available later in life when she has real issues that she needs to talk to you about.

But at the same time, you know her adorable, if sometimes erratic, little toddler phase won't last too long, and you want to be there to enjoy it. You're also tempted to swing in the other direction, and find a way to work part-time, or at least work from home on some days, so you can be more present in Zoe's early years. You know this would slow your career trajectory down. But you also know that more than 90 percent of mothers who spent less time at work for the sake of their kids were glad that they did so.[4]

Your friends who have kids (which is only about half of them so far) are pretty split on this. Of your close circle of mom friends, a few have found a way to throw themselves into their careers, a couple have figured out how to work shorter hours and don't mind appearing less ambitious, and a few are stay-at-home moms. Although they've all chosen different approaches, you love the support and lack of judgement among them. It makes you feel comfortable making the decision that is right for your family.

*If you choose to lean in to your job and hire a nanny to help with more of the childcare, go to **Chapter 31**.*

*If you choose to foster a better work/life balance by asking for a more flexible schedule, go to **Chapter 30**.*

19

MILKY VEIL

The epidural almost immediately curbs the pain. You are thankful for that and relax into a mildly uncomfortable waiting state. You even drift off to sleep a few times.

Five hours later, though, the doctor tells you that your baby's heart rate is slowing down, and you're not even fully dilated yet. You're going to need a C-section. At first you feel a pang of panic and despair—this was not your plan. But your mother and Anna both remind you that a healthy baby and healthy mom are the most important outcome here, and of course you agree. With 32 percent of women in the US having a cesarean delivery you are not alone in this experience.[1]

After the C-section, as you lie there with your healthy baby girl, Lily, on your chest, you think to yourself that it's ok. You are so grateful to experience this newfound, chest-bursting-with-emotion love. She is perfect.

Hours later, you find yourself filling out the form for Lily's birth certificate. Under the field that says "mother's name" you start to write your mother's name, and then you realize *you* are the mother! Although this is an identity you've been able to contemplate for the past seven and a half months (since you knew of your pregnancy), you feel a monumental life-shift in this moment. It both terrifies you and fulfills you beyond anything you have experienced.

The next few weeks are a blur. Lily has reflux, as about half of infants do, and cries more than you recall being warned about.[2] And you feel that your milk supply is insufficient, as is the reason for early weaning for 35 percent of women, so you try to pump in between feedings and drink herbal teas to try to increase it.[3] The result is a lifestyle in which you spend all of your waking hours thinking about breastmilk. Add to that the flushing of hormones through your system, and your reality becomes clouded under a milky veil.

Prior to Lily's birth, you talked to your professors about taking this semester's courses from home; you now attempt to do that. But a few weeks in, you realize that lack of sleep coupled with never having time to yourself to focus is preventing the success of this plan. You confirm with your student loan lender that you can take a semester off and still continue to receive your payments, and after confirming with your graduate school that you can continue your student health insurance during this time, you decide to take this semester off and resume your coursework in the spring. You know you'll be in debt for a long time, but at this point, you're more focused on day-to-day survival.

You start bundling up and going for walks each day with Lily strapped to you in a carrier. At first, just going around the block feels like an accomplishment, but soon you are able to walk a mile to the coffee shop and back, and you feel accomplished for this. You're also getting a chance to do more reading, and this reinvigorates your passion for learning. And you start to supplement Lily's feedings with formula. Once you get past the self-imposed guilt of it, you feel a large (approximately twenty ounces a day) weight lifted from you. Because

you've discovered that 53 percent of babies have formula intro-
duced into their diet by three months of age, you don't feel as
inadequate as you worried you would.[4]

*It is in this new reality that you continue on to **Chapter 24**.*

20

INTERVENE OR GIVE UP

Despite deciding to pull the protection on your honeymoon, you get your period on your second day back at work. Since the decision to have kids felt like such a giant mental leap, you actually feel a little surprised to realize you're not any more pregnant than you were before you jumped. But you know it's silly to expect it to happen so easily and plan to give it a go again this month.

After another two months of nonchalantly having hot sex right around the middle of your cycle, and then again feeling the let-down of a regularly scheduled menstrual cycle, you decide to get more intentional. You read a book called *Taking Charge of Your Fertility* and learn a lot about your body that you probably should have been taught in middle school, had your sex ed class focused on more than why to wear deodorant and how to put condoms on bananas.[1]

The guidance given in the book speaks directly to your love of data. You promptly download a fertility-tracking app and start taking your temperature first thing in the morning and logging it. Now you are able to accurately pinpoint when you're ovulating so that you can nonchalantly lure Nathan into hot, "spontaneous" sex at exactly the right time.

With each month that passes, your analytical precision improves. And with each new period, your level of disappointment skyrockets. Nathan stops falling for your charade of spontaneous love-making, since it only seems to happen once a month now, and you have become more demanding than cajoling. With this, he starts experiencing some performance anxiety, which makes the whole process even less pleasant. You are newlyweds and weren't even sure you wanted to have a baby yet. How did you become so desperately methodical so quickly?

After another six months of trying, you're getting pretty discouraged. You know from your obsessive internet research that 85 percent of couples have conceived by now, so you start to worry that there is something wrong with you.[2]

Or maybe with Nathan. You start your investigation with him. You quickly find out that not only does he have a healthy sperm count and mobility, but that he only needs two and a half minutes in a medical exam room with an adult magazine to confirm this.

After a few more months you go see your doctor. You do a series of tests involving dye, ultrasounds, and blood work. She doesn't see anything wrong with you and tells you to just keep trying.

But you're tired of trying! The emotional rollercoaster of getting your hopes up and then being let down, month after month, is taking its toll on your happiness. Your coworkers are starting to notice your distracted moodiness, and your friends, while supportive, are starting to get glazed looks in their eyes when you talk about your ovulation indicators.

You and Nathan talk it over and agree that this path just isn't sustainable for you right now. The stress and single-mindedness of it are wearing on you both. You discuss taking the next step toward trying to conceive and starting on fertility treatments. This would mean a lot of hormones and discomfort and a pretty large expense, even after the portion that your company would cover.

You also consider just stopping trying. You wouldn't try *not* to get pregnant; you'd just stop doing all the work to try to make it happen. No more temperature checks, no more planning work travel around ovulation, no more letting yourself be aware of where in your cycle you are. While it feels disappointing to give up, as you really do want a baby, it also sounds like a huge relief waiting around the corner.

After staring squinty-eyed in varying levels of light through teary eyes, trying to see a line that doesn't exist on another pregnancy test, you know you need to make a change.

If you decide to start down the road of fertility treatments, go to Chapter 26.

If you decide to intentionally stop trying to get pregnant, and just see what happens, go to Chapter 27.

21

HAPPILY EVER AFTER AS TWO

You open your eyes and look at the clock: 11:43 A.M. This makes sense since you don't think you fell asleep until close to 2:00 A.M., after the final stragglers from the hilarious and uncensored nine-bottle-of-wine dinner party you hosted last night said their good-byes. You groggily make your way down to the kitchen and put on coffee. Nathan has already gotten up and gone to the gym.

As you drink your coffee, you peruse Facebook on your phone. You see a few photos of the incredibly cute and well-behaved-appearing offspring of some of your close friends. For a minute, you have a twinge of envy. But then you look at the time stamp and see that most of them were posted over five hours ago when you were still in the midst of REM sleep. Your envy subsides.

You are trending to be like 14 percent of women in the US who go through their child-bearing years without bearing any children.[1] And more and more, you are feeling comfortable, and perhaps even vindicated, with this fact.

After a round of layoffs at your company resulted in your job being eliminated, you took your severance package and your experience and decided to start your own consulting business, helping small businesses with their marketing materials. This has given you the flexibility to dictate your own schedule, with enough advance planning. Nathan found a company to work for that gives him ample time off, and the two of you have been spending about four of those weeks traveling each year. Recently you have started planning a year-long sabbatical for both of you, in which you plan to work your way through Southeast Asia, writing a travel blog.

It's not that you never have doubts, and you and Nathan have revisited the baby decision a couple of times. Every time a colleague, or even a well-meaning, but unaware, friend, asks you when you're planning to procreate, you feel a mixture of uncertainty and defensiveness. After all, you do enjoy your friends' children, and you now have an amazing nephew that your brother Jonas and his wife Peggy recently brought into the world. You are happy for all of them, but you are also happy in your life.

You and Nathan go on to see some amazing places, grow to admirable heights in your careers, and build extremely close relationships with the eventual two nieces and one nephew that grace your collective families. You live happily ever after—in some ways just the two of you, but in more ways as part of a beautifully supportive and enriching web of family and friends.

The End

(Want to see what would have happened if you had tried to have children and then let nature take its course? Turn to Chapter 20 and make a different choice. Or if you've explored all the paths, turn to the Epilogue.)

22

BREAK THE CEILING OR BREAK OUT

After you decided to stay in your team lead role and set your sights on the next rung, the discontent that was plaguing you largely dissipated. You realize that spending so much time on that decision was keeping you from appreciating the great aspects of your job: you have a flexible (albeit time-consuming) schedule, a great team, and you're working on really interesting problems, even if you're not exactly changing the world.

Once you really focus on the work ahead of you, you start to have some ideas about how to scale the work your team is doing. You see that you could combine a few of the teams at your company to provide an end-to-end platform for financial management and that this initiative could massively increase revenue at your company over the next few years.

You bring the idea to your manager, Paul, and you are surprised by his unenthusiastic response. He has always seemed supportive of the work you are doing, but this is the first time you've brought a big idea to him that would change the strategy of your business. He tells you that it's a nice idea, but that the company isn't really set up to try something like that. Your confidence wavers.

A few weeks later, you get an email that makes your stomach churn. The VP of your division sends an org-wide note congratulating your boss on his innovative idea for restructuring your department to create better end-to-end financial tools for your customers. It's your idea, to a T.

You take the rest of the day off and sit on your couch ragecrying and eating french fries dipped in a chocolate milkshake while texting with your friend Simone about what happened. With puffy eyes and feeling vaguely sick to your stomach, you decide you have nothing to lose by confronting Paul.

In his office the next day, Paul looks you straight in the eye and tells you that it wasn't your idea; it was something he had been working on for months. You find that doubtful based on his initial reaction when you pitched the strategy to him.

You're tempted to go to his boss, the VP of your department, and let him know that this was your idea. Not purely out of vengeance, but because you believe that you would be a better person to execute it. If you could show your VP the whole strategy that you've been working on, maybe he would realize that you are the right person to lead the company in this new direction. But if you go to your VP and he doesn't decide to give you the opportunity, you'll just be stuck with a manager who is both conniving and mad at you for going over him.

You are equally tempted to just run and start over in that journalism career you have fantasized about. Why stick around and deal with dynamics like this again and again? They seem to loom ahead, blocking your way to the glass ceiling you have always heard about and are just now beginning to understand.

The part of you that is excited to run with your vision and take your company to the next level wants to stick around to do just that. The feminist in you wants to stick around too, if only to show guys like Paul that they can't get ahead with these antics. You know that only 6.4 percent of Fortune 500 companies are run by women, and you want to be part of the force that changes that.[1]

The jilted part of you wants to escape from this corrupt system now, while you still have your optimism somewhat intact.

If you decide to go to your VP and make a case for why your manager shouldn't be trusted and why you would be the right person to lead the strategy that you came up with, go to Chapter 32.

If you decide that this corporate dynamic isn't for you after all and decide to try to start over in a journalism career, go to Chapter 23.

23

RELOCATE OR STAY PUT

You start your search for a journalism career as advised by your favorite college English professor, who you recently got back in touch with for guidance. She told you to start writing as much as you can, find a niche, build up your social media presence, and then network like crazy. The networking piece definitely isn't your cup of tea, but you force yourself out of your comfort zone and follow her advice.

At one such networking event, pompously titled "the future of media and publishing," you are standing against the wall, laser-focused on your Campari spritz, when you look up and a handsome bearded guy is walking toward you with a big smile. "Chelsea!" he says and goes in for a hug. You hug him back and say, "Hi, my name isn't Chelsea." He realizes he just hugged Chelsea's apparent doppelgänger, backs off slightly, and blushes. You laugh and tell him it's fine . . . you needed a hug. He says his name is Forrest and asks if he can buy you a drink. Maybe this networking event isn't so bad after all.

You start hanging out with Forrest, and while things occasionally get physical, you really are not looking for a commitment. The two of you sit in coffee shops together, working on your writing. You are writing blog posts about current events in your neighborhood and are actually gaining a small following through Facebook and Nextdoor. And Forrest, who already has a job at the news desk of the local paper, is trying to break into writing his own column, so he is working on his op-ed samples.

You start to get some requests to republish your blog posts, and your networking efforts have paid off: you know more and more people in the news and publishing world. You feel like you're slowly losing touch with many of your old friends from your corporate gig—which almost feels like a different lifetime, even though you only left six months ago—and replacing them with new, edgier ones. It's kind of exciting.

You and Forrest become more of an official couple, showing up to parties together and sleeping at each other's apartments a few nights a week. It's been so long since you let yourself feel the giddiness of a new relationship. You try to be aloof and skeptical at first, but you get pulled under by the chemistry and excitement of the whole thing. Forrest is a riveting conversationalist and a knee-weakening lover at a time in your life where you feel you finally have a refined palate for both.

Through the connections you've made, some career opportunities start to present themselves. Not a moment too soon either. You've been quickly working your way through your savings to pay your bills between jobs, and the end of your year of affordable health insurance is closing in on you.

The traction you've gained with your neighborhood blog has gotten you an interview for a job as a clerk and reporter for the regional section of a weekly independent paper. It would only be a part-time job, but taking it would give you the flexibility to pursue freelance writing work at the same time. You think that could be an interesting starting point for your new career trajectory.

You also hear of an opportunity with a local internet company; you'd be writing reviews of different neighborhoods for them to show on their website. You apply to that, too, and feel pretty confident that one of these roles will pan out.

With these developments, you're thinking you have a plan, but then you hear about what could be a life-changing opportunity. A woman who you met through one of your networking circles has just turned down a job as a journalist and editor for a tourism publication in Bangalore, India, and asks if you'd like her to refer you. The chance to live abroad sounds intriguing, and you don't think you'd be likely to find another opportunity with so much scope of responsibility in a new field. You figure you don't have anything to lose by applying, so you accept her kind offer and send in your portfolio.

Within a few weeks, you have interviewed for all three roles. You first hear from the recruiter from the internet company, who mispronounces your name and tells you they have extended an offer to another candidate. You feel dejected.

But then you receive offers from both the weekly newspaper and the Bangalore tourism publication! You and Forrest go out for drinks to celebrate your options. And suddenly you find yourself on the opposite side of the decision you had to make in your relationship with Nathan years ago: you have a compelling reason to relocate for work, and your boyfriend is staying put.

You have fallen for Forrest and struggle to imagine life without him. He says he loves you too, but he feels rooted in his community and his work and doesn't feel open to moving. You have to admit that you have also come to feel rooted in this community. Staying here and taking the job at the weekly paper, while working on your freelance writing career, feels like a safe and comfortable option. That said, with a freelancer's salary and no job-provided health insurance, the comfort would be only emotional; you would be scraping by for the foreseeable future.

The chance to move to India while working as a journalist and editor feels like an opportunity that may never come your way again. You're almost thirty and will likely want to settle down and have kids in this next decade of your life. You don't want to regret never having the chance to do something scary and crazy like this before you do.

If you choose to stay put with Forrest and take the local writing jobs, go to *Chapter 33.*

If you choose to say goodbye to Forrest and move to India for work, go to *Chapter 29.*

24

CLOSE TO FAMILY OR MAKE IT ALONE

A woman in your master's program has also had a baby recently, and the two of you decide to share a part-time nanny so you can both go back to school. This requires some additional student loans, which start to feel abstract as you can't imagine ever being able to fully pay them off. But the situation works well enough for the short term, and you are finally able to finish your last semester of graduate school.

You walk in your graduation ceremony, feeling an acute sense of accomplishment as you look out and see Lily sitting on your mother's lap, chewing on a plastic pony. The past year and a half have been some of the most trying times you have been through, and you let yourself feel proud of how far you and Lily have come.

Your last semester at school further solidified your passion for solving social issues through technology, and you are excited to find a job where you can further this pursuit. There are some very promising job prospects in the city where you live, and you start applying to them.

You also have a long talk with your mother about what comes next. She would love to help out with Lily and play an active role in your lives, but she doesn't want to leave her home and her community, which is a two-hour drive away. If you were to move back to your hometown, you'd have her there waiting to help you. But you know the job prospects will be fewer and less cutting edge than what you can find in the city.

It's not that you require your mother to watch Lily during the day—you can find a nanny or daycare for that, although doing so will definitely make expenses tight. Given that childcare in the US is, in some places, more expensive than college, this is a serious concern.[1] More importantly, this past year has made you acutely aware of how small of a support system you have around you and how much you could use one. You have plenty of friends who care about you and say they're there to help out. But at the end of the day, they are out living their own lives, and you are trying not to drown in yours.

Making the decision to prioritize proximity to your mother over exciting work prospects wouldn't be an unusual one. Americans live a median distance of eighteen miles from their mother, and 80 percent live within a two-hour drive. One of the biggest reasons for this is that they want support when they are raising children.[2] You always thought you'd want to move far away from home when you were out of the house, but now that you have Lily, you can understand this phenomenon much better.

If you choose to find your dream job in the city and go it alone without parental support, go to Chapter 40.

If you choose to move back to your hometown to be closer to your mother, go to Chapter 43.

25

HAPPILY EVER AFTER RAISING A KID

Your first year staying home with Zoe feels a bit isolating. You can read *Goodnight Moon* and *Bear on a Bike* (both of which you now know by heart) only so many times before you start to doubt your own sanity.

But once Zoe turns two and you are able to sign up for a co-op preschool, your decision to stay home begins to feel more sound. You have made a close community of mom friends and take turns hosting play dates and going on outings together. There is a little drama in the group from time to time, but it keeps things interesting.

As Zoe enters kindergarten, you consider going back to work again, but none of the other moms are doing so, and you're not really feeling a strong drive to uproot your routines. Plus, you've finally gotten to the point where you can have a few hours to yourself during the day and think that maybe now you can start that parenting blog you've been mentally writing posts for.

Silas has gotten a couple of promotions and is now running corporate partnerships at his employee assistance program gig, so you're not so stressed about finances anymore. He's not around as much, but you've gotten used to that, and you two still get out on date nights every other Saturday. Zoe is a riot to be around; you think she might end up being a Broadway performer, the way she sings and dances for any audience she can find.

You start taking a kickboxing class, get a puppy, join the school auction committee, and live happily ever after as a stay-at-home mom.

The End

(Want to see what would have happened if you took the working mother path instead? Turn back to Chapter 16 and make a different choice. Or if you've explored all the paths, turn to the Epilogue.)

26

CAN'T CONTROL EVERYTHING

You and Nathan get a recommendation for a fertility specialist and make your first appointment. After a series of tests, some of them redundant to what your doctor has already done, you are advised to start with some hormone therapy medications and an intrauterine insemination (IUI).[1] You go ahead with this plan. The process isn't horrible, although the hormones do make you feel moodier than you already did. But it also doesn't work . . . four cycles in a row.

Your fertility doctor tells you that your next option is in vitro fertilization (IVF).[2]

You set out to prepare yourself for this final spin around the mentally and physically exhausting roulette wheel. You read a book about IVF, comb through online forums, and start a series of acupuncture treatments to prepare your body for what lies ahead.

Finally, you start your first IVF cycle. Nathan gets trained in mixing and administering your stem injections, and you sit on the couch watching old *Sex in the City* episodes to take your mind off the pain. This process lasts for two weeks, during which time you become increasingly bloated, tired, and irritable. Or, more accurately, you're unable to wear normal pants, unable to stay awake, and unable to keep from crying about everything. Your outside feels like a swollen battleground from all of your injections, and your inside feels like an over-worked egg factory.

On the day of your egg retrieval, you are the most nervous you can ever remember being. But the surgery goes well, and you go home to rest, with eighteen fewer eggs in your ovaries than you woke up with that morning. Now you recover and wait. You've taken the past week and a half off of work and will need to go back in a few days.

One afternoon at work, you get the call from your doctor that you've been waiting for. Four of the embryos were successfully fertilized. You take the rest of the day off, because you're unable to concentrate due to nervousness and excitement. After doing some research, you learn that your odds of getting pregnant are actually worse if you plant two embryos versus one, so you plan to implant one and freeze the other three.[3]

The egg implanting is fairly painless compared to all the other turmoil your body has been through lately. But the wait is excruciating. You start peeing on sticks only three days later, which, unsurprisingly, doesn't produce any results. But a few days after that, you start to see a faint line. And it keeps getting darker every day that you check. You are ecstatic.

But when you go in for your first ultrasound two weeks later, there is no heartbeat and only an empty placenta. You have miscarried, as is the case for 22 percent of IVF pregnancies.[4] You cry the whole way home and well into the following day. After that, you just feel numb.

But you pick yourself up again, and three months later, you try again to implant one of the frozen embryos. This time you don't even get a positive pregnancy test.

Later in the year, right after your thirty-first birthday, you try one final attempt. Your body is worn out, you are twenty pounds over your usual weight from all of the medications and the lack of mobility you've been experiencing. You know this is your final attempt. Not only will this use up what is left of your lifetime fertility insurance coverage and your savings, but you just don't have it in you to keep going beyond this.

Emotionally, perhaps you had already given up. Or perhaps your body was too unstable after so much struggle. Whatever the case, you finish your long, taxing journey through infertility treatments with no baby in your uterus and no more hope in your heart.

• • •

The next year is hard. A distance has grown between you and Nathan that feels palpable as you both mourn in your own unique ways. It seems that friends are announcing pregnancies with comical frequency. And it takes almost that full year to get your body back to normal and get your mind back to work, friends, hobbies, and anything other than conception.

But you do slowly start to emerge from the mourning period. At first a good day is just getting out of bed the first time your alarm goes off and making it through the morning without crying. Then you start saying yes to dinners out with your friends. Finally, you're even able to show up to a close friend's baby shower without feeling miserable. You and Nathan get a dog: a pug named Maurice. And you start taking trips together, which reminds you of the joys that you used to experience in life, before what will become known to you as "the dark years."

*You even start to find joy and appreciation at times for the freedom and flexibility that your life without children affords you. And as you do, you go to **Chapter 21**.*

27

DOUBLE DOWN OR ONLY CHILD

Your life became so much more enjoyable once you pulled yourself out of the cycle of obsessive procreation attempts. You and Nathan were able to find pleasure in each other again—both in terms of non-fertility conversation topics, and even in sex, purely for the sake of enjoyment.

After a year of this reignited partnership, and many an agendaless romp in the sheets, you are actually taken by surprise to realize that your period is late. Really late. You feel sick and tired, and completely overjoyed.

Other than a draining first trimester, your pregnancy goes smoothly. You are still working at the green energy company, having moved up to a marketing manager position. Your manager has children too, and she is supportive of you taking your full three-month maternity leave and then easing back in part-time for a few weeks. You recognize with disgust that this pales in comparison to other countries, with the US being the only high-income country in the world that does not offer paid maternity leave.[1] But you also know that a quarter of new mothers in the US have to go back to work ten days after having a baby, so you count your blessings.[2]

You work up until the baby comes . . . literally. You are sitting at your desk one morning, six days before your due date, when you feel a rush of liquid. You are one of the lucky 15 percent of women whose water breaks before you are even in labor . . . just like in the movies.[3] You somehow leave work and get to the hospital and proceed to have the medicated birth you had planned for.

You have a gorgeous little boy, and it feels like a distant dream has come true. You and Nathan decide to name him Paxton.

Your maternity leave passes in a haze of nursing, diapers, one-handed meals, occasional showers and laundry, and sheer and utter love. You are at the same time no longer yourself and more yourself than you have ever been. Your life is now a dichotomy of sensations. Everything that was ever enjoyable isn't anymore, and everything that was ever mundane is now fascinating.

When it is time to return to work, you enroll Paxton in an at-home daycare near your house. It feels heart-wrenching leaving him, but you trust that he is in good hands. After a couple of weeks of frequent crying over the humming "shlurp-chuckaah . . . shlurpchuckaah . . . shlurpchuckaah" sound of your breast pump, you get into a routine that works. Other than some pretty major sleep deprivation, you feel mostly back on your game at work. Paxton is growing at a healthy rate. And Nathan is making himself helpful where he can, although Paxton seems to only want you and your milk dispensary most of the time.

As you near Paxton's first birthday, your monthly cycle comes back. This prompts a conversation with Nathan: should you go on birth control or leave the possibilities open for a second child? You both had siblings and appreciated how you always had someone to be with as you grew up. You also both believe it would be good for Paxton to learn how to share and compromise and not get spoiled by being an only child. With women in the US having an average of 2.07 children, it certainly wouldn't be uncommon for you to try for another child.[4]

However, you've also learned that kids are expensive! Between the medical costs, the lost salary due to maternity leave, and daycare tuition, the first year alone has completely changed your lifestyle. You could find a way to make ends meet with two, but it would be tight.

You know from your first time attempting to get pregnant that it can take a long time. And if you did have two children, you would like them to be close enough in age to play together. But at the same time, you feel like you're just barely starting to get your body, and your sleep schedule, back since Paxton was born. You're not sure you're ready to dive back in again.

If you choose to go on birth control and stop while you're ahead, go to Chapter 41.

If you choose to try for another baby so that Paxton has a sibling to grow up with, go to Chapter 39.

28

RESIST TEMPTATION OR SUCCUMB

You open your laptop as the train speeds away from the station and power up your personal hotspot to catch up on emails. You just had to flee another teary daycare drop-off in order to catch the last express train, and your heart is still hurting from seeing Zoe's scrunched up little face as you ran for the door. You know from her teachers that she recovers within a few minutes of these goodbyes, but it leaves you shaken for longer than that.

As you absorb yourself in your work, though, the mom guilt fades away and the problem-solving part of your brain takes over. You have found a great job at a nonprofit that connects other nonprofits with technical volunteers, and you love the work you are doing. It leverages your vision for using technology to help solve social issues, and you're connecting with so many amazing people in both the public and private sectors through this work. As you anticipated, the pay is not that much more than daycare tuition. But the level of job satisfaction is high and you believe there are some great opportunities to grow in this role. Taking even a five-year break from your career would have cost you 19 percent of your lifetime earnings, which makes your decision to get a job more lucrative.[1]

Your days, while full of all of the goodness that a fulfilling job and a loving family provides, do not contain quite as many hours as you need. You do manage to fit the logistical part of mothering—like filling out school photo forms and scheduling doctor check-ups—into your work schedule. You rush home, spend a couple of preciously chaotic hours feeding, playing with, and bathing Zoe, and then put her to bed. Then you hop back online to catch up on work before you pass out yourself.

This works ok in terms of staying on top of your job and being a decent mother, but you're pretty sure you're getting a D– in the attentive wife and self-care departments, although you're not even sure that Silas has noticed your sub-par marital performance as he's not around much himself. He has had to do a fair amount of work travel as he ramps new corporate clients up on the employee assistance services his company provides. And when he is home, he seems pretty wiped out and just wants to sit and watch TV. With every click of the remote control, you feel more isolated in your own balancing act. Your resentment builds.

You start finding solitude from the chaos of life in small moments at the office. The cup of coffee you pour yourself before sitting down at your desk in the morning. The time flipping through Instagram while waiting for the elevator. And funny conversations with coworkers that have nothing to do with potty-training or yard maintenance.

You have one such coworker who is always good for a chat or a laugh: Jonathan from Accounting. Every time you bump into him you end up lingering a little bit, as he gives you his undivided attention and a charming smile. You recognize that the dynamic between you is a little flirty, but you don't feel bad about that—he's married too, and its harmless banter. It has just been so long since a man has acted flirtatiously with you, and you're having fun.

The thing you do feel a little guilty about is thinking of Jonathan during sex with Silas. You know that's probably not the sign of a healthy marriage. But at the same time, you haven't had any libido since Zoe was born, so if thinking about Jonathan is what gets your and Silas's sex life back on track, maybe there's no harm in that.

• • •

Life goes on in this precariously balanced state for fourteen more months. You scramble to stay on top of work and parenting. Zoe gets more and more comfortable with daycare and is staying up a little later, so you get some more time with her in the evenings. And you and Silas keep a distant but functional partnership. The most exciting parts of your day are often your strategically timed run-ins with Jonathan at the coffee maker or Slack conversations with him that start out as accounting questions and end up in whimsical banter.

You and Jonathan start emailing each other, sharing office gossip and funny memes. Pretty soon, you find yourself compulsively checking your phone in the evenings and on weekends, hoping for a note from him. You feel guilty each time you do, as you recognize that it is taking your attention away from Zoe. But you can't resist the dopamine rush you get from those little digital hits.

Then one day, your time of reckoning comes. You are on an overnight work trip with several co-workers, meeting with a company eight hours away that is interested in creating a technical volunteering program for their employees. After a work dinner, everyone heads to the bar. You say that you're tired and head up to your room; you are genuinely excited to get an uninterrupted night's sleep in a hotel room!

Jonathan follows you to the elevators. Out of the context of the office, he looks even sexier, and your heart pounds with the realization that you might actually have the opportunity for your fantasies to be realized here, in this corporate, beige Hilton. He touches your arm lightly and asks, "Do you want me to come up with you?"

Your entire life hits you in a flash. You feel terrified and guilty for how far you've let things go with Jonathan. All of the emails and flirty chats and Slack messages . . . you suddenly see the slippery slope you've been letting yourself slide down. If you keep sliding, you could crash and hurt everyone you care about—including yourself.

Through the fear and the guilt and the shame, you feel an even more powerful sensation: extreme lust. You look into Jonathan's eyes and feel an animal urge to tear his clothes off and devour him. You could do just that—no one would have to know. You're not alone in this desire: 13 percent of woman have sex with someone other than their spouse when married (still less than the 20 percent of married men).[2]

Except that you would know, and you know yourself: you are not someone who is able to compartmentalize your feelings.

Jonathan's hand slides behind your back, and he gives you an inquisitive smile.

If you decide to let your desire call the shots and bring Jonathan up to your room to live out your fantasies, regardless of the repercussions, go to Chapter 37.

If you decide to tell Jonathan you can't do this and make some lifestyle changes to alter the dangerous course you've been going down, go to Chapter 35.

29

HAPPILY EVER AFTER WORKING ABROAD

Your first several months in Bangalore make you wonder if you've made a terrible mistake. You feel crushed by longing for Forrest, overwhelmed by the constant noises, smells, and visuals that are so new to your senses, and—although the publication you are working for is all in English, and many around you are able to speak English—most people outside of the office do not, and you feel lost among a sea of people whose words you do not understand.

As you get your bearings, though, these feelings of loneliness and over-stimulation give way to feelings of wonder and excitement. Your job forces you to get to know this new city intimately so that you can write about the unique experiences and hidden gems that visitors should seek out. The demands of a tourism journalist force you to explore beyond your comfort zone, and you to get to know some amazing people in the process. On any given day you might find yourself getting a chiropractic foot treatment followed by a basement meal of fish omelets, learning about meditation practices in an ancient Hindu temple, or taking a rickshaw ride between art galleries.

You start to make friends too. Some of them are ex-pats who moved to Bangalore in search of new experiences and cultures, as you did. But slowly you are able to make headway with making local friends too—people who have lived their whole lives in this area and are now working tech jobs in the city. Before long, you feel confident and happy in your new home.

You end up starting your own publication after a few years, covering local arts and culture. You meet a wonderful man from London named Alex, who is working in Bangalore as a quality assurance manager, and eventually, you end up marrying him, have three children, move to a suburb outside the city, and live happily ever after working abroad.

The End

(Want to see what would have happened if you stayed with Forrest and took the weekly newspaper job instead? Turn back to Chapter 23 and make a different choice. Or if you've explored all the paths, turn to the Epilogue.)

30

PRIORITIZE HIS NEEDS OR HERS

You requested to work from home two days a week, and to your surprise, had your request granted by your manager. You are now like 45 percent of employed Americans who work remotely at least part of the time.[1]

That added flexibility, however, has ironically increased your time commitments. You have started taking Mom and Me swim classes with Zoe on Friday afternoons now that you're available to. And you have found that using that extra time at home to do quick chores like a load of laundry and running to pick up more milk, while still staying on top of your work, has increased your day-to-day responsibilities even more. Still, you are grateful for having the extra time with Zoe.

You are the only one on your team who is working remotely part of the time, and that has given you somewhat of a complex. You know you're staying on top of your work, and you are calling into meetings on your remote days. But you can't help but feel insecure that you are being judged as a slacker. That insecurity is fueling increased efforts on your part, and you find yourself spending more and more evenings going above and beyond to prove yourself.

Between your increased time with Zoe and your increased efforts to prove yourself at work, you are ending up with no time for Silas. In fact, you, like 30 percent of couples with kids, haven't had a date night in more than six months.[2] You feel bad that you haven't been getting any quality time together, and you feel even worse that you're not exactly longing for that time. You want to spend precious time with Zoe—she is doing new amazing things every day—and you want to be great at your job and make the world a little better through your work, and you want a couple of minutes to yourself once in a while!

Silas confides in you one night that he feels lonely and unappreciated—even a little in the way—in your relationship. You know it's callous of you, but the only reaction you have is resentment. You've been working so hard, are making life-altering sacrifices for your sweet daughter, and you haven't slept through the night in over a year . . . and his biggest complaint is that he doesn't feel appreciated enough? You roll your eyes and say you're sorry he's feeling that way, and that maybe you can talk about it next time you have some time together.

Silas suggests that you plan a date night so that you actually *can* spend some time together. You're happy to do that in theory, but you don't have family in town (Silas's parents went south for the winter), you're trying to watch your expenses since daycare costs so much, and honestly, you're just exhausted by the time evening rolls around. You don't exactly feel like getting out of your sweats and off the couch on a Saturday night.

You feel torn between living the lifestyle that is calling you right now—one focused on Zoe, work, and getting rest where you can—and living the lifestyle that your marriage is clearly asking for—namely making some compromises in order to reconnect with Silas.

*If you decide that you don't have the capacity for more than Zoe, work, and basic self-care and that you can bond more with Silas later, go to **Chapter 36**.*

*If you decide to get some extra date nights, show some extra affection, and reinvest in your relationship with Silas, go to **Chapter 38**.*

31

AUTHENTIC OR PROFESSIONAL

Since hiring your nanny, Faith, to help with taking Zoe to and from preschool, you've had just enough extra time at work to feel less rushed and get a little more face time in. And you have found that the time you are missing with Zoe during these transitions wasn't really quality time anyway. You still get to spend time with her most mornings and evenings, and feeling more on top of your job has freed up your mental load so that you can be more present with her.

But it also means an extra monthly expense, so you are hoping that your investment pays off with a steeper career trajectory. You bring this aspiration up with your manager during one of your annual performance reviews.

Your manager, Michael, tells you that you've been doing great and that he thinks you could be on track for a promotion soon. Your company has recently acquired a couple of international office supply brands, and there will be room for growth and expanded scope.

However, he tells you, if you have aspirations of moving up the leadership ladder, you will need to work on your "executive presence." He goes on to say that you can come across as being overly emotional, abrasive, and bossy. And also, leaders in the company tend to wear more formal clothing and present themselves more professionally. Although this is true, he fails to mention that the people who dress more formally have client-facing roles, which you do not. You've always been more of a jeans-and-t-shirt girl.

You feel deflated. You've been doing great work, and you feel that you're being held back by squishy personality feedback. Many of your male counterparts are much more contentious and argumentative than you are, and you see them progressing in their careers despite that—or maybe even because of it. This is a dynamic that many women experience, as women are 1.4 times more likely to receive critical subjective feedback on their performance reviews than men.[1]

You've never been asked to modify your personality or appearance before, and at first, the request feels at odds with your core belief system. You are vocal and passionate about your work because you care about it, and because that's how you communicate. The idea of getting dressed up in clothes that don't feel like you and taming your communication style to be more in line with what your company—or at least your manager—prefers, feels like you're compromising who you are. Your suspicion that you wouldn't be getting this same feedback if you were a man makes the request even harder to stomach.

You could keep going as you are—wearing the clothes that feel comfortable to you and speaking your mind in the way that feels natural. Your job is not at risk, but it sounds like your career trajectory could be.

Or you could take the feedback that Michael gave you and make some changes. You could go out and buy a new work wardrobe and start carrying yourself differently. Maybe you could even work with a coach to help you build that executive presence that you have been encouraged to pursue. It doesn't feel very authentic, but you know you could do it. You do want to continue growing in your career.

If you choose to be authentic to yourself and not conform to the corporate professional norm, go to Chapter 46.

If you decide to step up your game and adopt a professional persona, go to Chapter 44.

32

HAPPILY EVER AFTER
AT THE TOP

You are still shaking as you step onto the elevator. You have just come from "the meeting" with the VP of your department, Mitchell Browne, where you pitched to him the idea of you running the new department that is forming.

Although you were tempted to throw your manager Paul under the bus, a couple of informal mentors that you have built relationships with told you that this would only make you look unprofessional and untrustworthy, and that you should focus instead on your own ideas and strengths. Since the full plan hadn't been rolled out yet, you went in to the meeting with Mitchell and presented the work you had done over the past several months to outline the strategy for combining departments and building an end-to-end solution, as though your manager hadn't already pitched it to him. You also directly told him that you would like to step into a larger leadership role to drive the execution of this strategy.

Mitchell seemed impressed with the details you had worked through, and you felt that you presented your case well, after rehearsing it numerous times in front of the bathroom mirror, but he said that he would need to think about where you could contribute since your manager was already on point to run this.

You barely sleep the night after that conversation, running all of the details of what you said and scenarios of what could happen through your spinning mind. It turns out that losing sleep that night was fruitless because it takes two weeks for your VP to get back to you. By then, you've already assumed the worst, grieved, and arrived at a steady state of disappointment.

Despite the mental games you have played with yourself, the news is remarkably good! Although Mitchell doesn't decide to circumvent Paul and put you in charge of the project, he was impressed with your strategic thinking and your initiative, and he asks if you would like to apply for a new director role that is opening up under him, running customer acquisition strategy.

You interview for that role and get the offer. Since you were woefully unaware of how to negotiate your salary in past job offers, like 68 percent of women in the US, you take a stab at negotiating this time around.[1] Your tactics are successful, and you land yourself a 15 percent raise as part of this promotion.

You stumble a few times, but overall prove yourself to be a valuable leader in this new role. A year later, when enough other employees *do* throw Paul under the bus for taking their ideas, not giving them credit, and generally being an unsupportive manager, he ends up exiting the company to pursue other opportunities. You are the clear choice to backfill his role, and you move to become the senior director of the organization that you originally thought up.

You have several more successful years at the bank and then take a job offer as VP of marketing for a media outlet. As you rise further in your career, you find that you have more time to give back—you start mentoring young women in their careers and do some pro-bono marketing for a local foodbank. You meet a lovely man named Phillip at the insurance agency; you enjoy his cooking and sense of humor enough to eventually move in with him.

You spend seven enjoyable years together, and two less-enjoyable ones, before you decide to break it off with Phillip. You continue to rise in your career to chief marketing officer, join a couple of nonprofit and corporate boards, enjoy a weekly Sunday morning brunch with a close group of girlfriends, and live happily ever after at the top.

The End

*(Want to see what would have happened if you had switched to a journalism career instead of climbing the corporate ladder? Turn back to **Chapter 22** and make a different choice. Or if you've explored all the paths, turn to the **Epilogue**.)*

33

HIS NAME OR YOURS

Staying rooted feels like a good decision, and you're not driving yourself crazy over what could have been. The staff at the weekly paper is pretty cool, and you're enjoying your time there. It's only been a few months since you began writing the local news column, and your editor is already talking with you about expanding your beat to cover some event reviews.

Forrest is so relieved that you stayed; he's even showing more signs of settling down with you. He updated his Facebook status to "in a relationship" and brought a toothbrush and a change of clothes to keep at your apartment. Sure, you have plenty of friends who have already shacked up, walked down the aisle, and started a family, but that green toothbrush that is now in your bathroom is giving you a sense of commitment that is both exciting and intimidating.

• • •

The winter starts to melt away and the blossoms of spring inspire you to plan a little vacation for you and Forrest. You decide it would be cute to visit the town you grew up in—it's beautiful in the spring, and you'd like to show him more of your upbringing. Plus, you're long overdue for a visit with both of your parents. You decide to stay in a bed and breakfast there, both for privacy, and so you don't have to choose between parents' houses.

Much of your hometown has changed beyond recognition as a new generation has moved in. But you're still able to find several of your old haunts, and you even run into a couple of high school friends who never left. It feels like an intimate show-and-tell session with Forrest, and you are loving it.

On the last night of your trip, cozied up in front of the fireplace in your B&B room, Forrest turns to you. "I've been thinking a lot, and I don't think I've ever felt this way about anyone before. You make me so happy, and I'm wondering if you would spend the rest of your life with me?" It takes a second to realize what he's saying . . . "Did you just ask me to marry you?" you ask. "I think so," he says.

This wasn't the traditional speech you expected in your younger years, but it's exactly what you would expect from Forrest. And you love him for it. "Let's do it!" you tell him, and you tear off each other's clothes to seal the deal.

• • •

The next several months are an exciting execution of to-do lists. Before planning the wedding, you both decide that you should consolidate apartments. You want to make sure you're good at living together and you know you can save money by combining rent payments. Since you've both been living in one-bedrooms, and you both like to be able to write at home, you decide a two-bedroom will be necessary. After combing the city and wasting several hundred dollars on rental application fees, you end up in a cozy apartment overlooking a park, with a large bedroom and an office.

Now that you're shacked up, you pull up the next to-do list: wedding planning. You decide on an intimate ceremony in a rose garden followed by a celebration at the art museum banquet facility. You start planning the event for the next summer.

Decent job: check. Apartment: check. Wedding logistics: check. You've got this major life change all under control. Until Forrest casually utters two little words: "Mrs. Bellamy." You look up: "What did you just say?" you ask. "Oh, just trying out how your new name will sound!" he answers.

It turns out you two had very different assumptions about a name change. You had figured that you would just keep your maiden name, since you're already in your thirties and you've started to make a name for yourself with your writing. And you *like* your name as it is!

Forrest, while very progressive and even edgy in so many ways, turns out to be traditional in his view of marital name changes. He believes that if a woman doesn't change her last name when she gets married, it means she's not really committed and wants to keep an out. His parents, you find out, share this same belief system.

Although your beliefs are in the minority, they're not obscure. About 20 percent of women in the US keep their maiden names.[1] You want Forrest to know how fully into this marriage you are, but the feminist in you is having a hard time backing down on this decision. Apparently, one study found that 63 percent of men polled would be upset if their wives kept their maiden names, although you had no idea that of all of the major life choices you've faced in recent years, this would be a significant point of resistance.[2]

The weekend after you encounter this hiccup, you have a girls' getaway at your friend Mara's family's cabin, and you mention the last name debacle. Although the friends present who are married are pretty split on what they did with their names, they all unanimously agree that it should be your decision, and that you shouldn't be guilted into changing your last name if you don't want to. You tend to agree with them, but at the same time you want to make Forrest happy.

If you decide to hold firm on your principles and desires and keep your maiden name, go to Chapter 34.

If you decide to compromise your wishes in order to make your fiancé feel happy and secure, go to Chapter 42.

34

HAPPILY EVER AFTER DODGING A BULLET

With the words of your friends giving you confidence, you sit Forrest down one evening to let him know that you've decided to keep your own name. You tell him that it has nothing to do with your love or commitment to him, but that you feel like you've worked hard to establish a professional name for yourself and you want to keep it. You are completely shocked by his reaction as he yells something about how he can't even trust you and that you don't care about him, and he storms out of the apartment.

You call your mother in tears. This isn't the Forrest you know and love. She is surprised too and doesn't have any great suggestions.

Four hours later, Forrest stumbles in the front door. He seems drunk. Even though you had been lying in bed waiting up for him, you pretend to be sleeping so that you don't have to talk with him in this state. You listen to him clang around for a while, then he drifts off to sleep snoring.

The next morning Forrest is extremely apologetic. He explains that he has some trust issues from his last relationship and says he will never let his temper get the best of him again. After some further discussion, you forgive him and keep going, ready to put that whole incident behind you.

A month later, though, that temper flares again. This time he is triggered by you wanting to go out of town for your friend Sherry's bachelorette party. He gets jealous, makes accusations, and ultimately brings up the last name issue again. You've never been with a man who had a temper before, and it freaks you out.

You talk the situation over with your friends over margaritas at the bachelorette weekend. The story brings up experiences that a couple of your friends share, about partners they have had in the past who became verbally abusive. No one tells you not to worry about it—they are all concerned.

As you near your wedding date, Forrest continues to show signs of a short fuse. You can't stop the nagging feeling that you don't fully know him and that you might be rushing into this marriage.

After some more deep discussions with your friends and your mother, you decide to broach the subject with Forrest. You tell him that you love him, but you feel like you need more time with him before you feel fully confident in making a life-long commitment to him. You confide that his outbursts have left you shaken and uncertain.

In reaction to this, Forrest blows his lid. He yells, he cries, he calls you the most horrific names, he gets so close in your face that you feel fear running through you. This is the validation you needed.

When Forrest comes back apologizing the next day, you don't give in. You tell him that you want to call off the wedding, and you leave your apartment with two suitcases of your belongings. After a few weeks of staying on friends' couches, you tell Forrest that you want to take your name off the lease so that you can find your own place. He begs you to reconsider but, although you are heartbroken, you are firm in your resolve. You know you are not alone, and you are proud of yourself for getting out when you did, as almost half of all women in the US experience psychological aggression from an intimate partner, and of those, half have had experiences escalate to severe physical violence.[1]

Time heals your heartache and solidifies the feeling that you made the right decision. You continue your journey surrounded by friends and loved ones who don't lash out at you over their own insecurities, and you live happily ever after having dodged a bullet.

The End

*(Want to see what would have happened if you had decided to take Forrest's name? Turn back to **Chapter 33** and make a different choice. Or if you've explored all the paths, turn to the Epilogue.)*

35

HAPPILY EVER AFTER WALKING THE LINE

You sit shaking in your hotel room. You've just told Jonathan that you can't do this—any of it. You know it was the right decision, but you can't help but feel a sense of loss and disappointment.

Back home after your work trip, you try to refocus. You try to be more in the moment with Zoe and Silas when you are home and more focused on your assignments when you are at work.

You receive a few emails from Jonathan—they start off playful and casual, but progressively turn more concerned. "Why aren't you responding to me? Are you mad? I miss our connection." You have set your resolve to end this emotional affair, and you are not going to slide backward. You don't reply, and you go out of your way to avoid him at work. But still you miss him, and it hurts.

After a couple of months of cutting off contact with Jonathan, you realize that you're not bouncing back as you had hoped. After some soul searching, you believe the reason for this is that the void between you and Silas—which might have been part of the reason you let your emotions stray, to begin with—still hasn't been filled.

The way you two ended up together originally wasn't as intentional or as romantic as you would have choreographed. You didn't have a lot of time to bond and grow as a couple before becoming parents. And the taxing nature of caring for a baby—now a toddler—takes its toll on even the strongest of relationships.

You bring up the idea of couples counseling with Silas, and he skeptically agrees. It starts out a little forced and awkward as you learn to communicate about your underlying issues in healthy and productive ways. But you uncover a lot and find a new level of honesty and compassion with each other. After about a year of weekly counseling sessions—fully covered by Silas's benefits package, fortunately—you feel that you have built a new, stronger foundation for your marriage.

Your close bout with infidelity, and the subsequent repair process, has scared you into avoiding temptation more intentionally going forward. You have too much to lose.

A year later, when your good friend Laura confides in you that she is feeling tempted to cheat on her wife with a woman on her soccer team, you are able to share your close call with her, and the steps you took to mitigate it. Laura and her wife start going to counseling earlier than you did, and you are glad that you were able to spare her some of the anguish you went through.

You and Silas still hit bumpy patches in your relationship going forward. But now you have the communication tools and the confidence to push through it. With that, and a good community of friends to lean on through the harder times, you and Silas live happily ever after walking the line.

The End

(Want to see what would have happened if you had given in to temptation with Jonathan? Turn back to Chapter 28 and make a different choice. Or if you've explored all the paths, turn to the Epilogue.)

36

FORGIVE OR FORGET

For a while, your problem with Silas wanting more of your time and attention seems to have resolved itself. Or rather, the absence of further complaining on his end, coupled with the water-treading you go through as part of your daily life, puts the issue out of your mind. Life goes on in the whirlwind routine that you have become accustomed to.

Slowly, though, you start to notice that Silas isn't around as much. He's still home most evenings and weekends, but he doesn't really seem to be there. He's spending a lot of time on his laptop or looking at his phone. He doesn't hang around as you're feeding or playing with Zoe or watching TV after she's asleep the way he used to.

Then he starts to spend more evenings having to stay late at work. In the small amount of bandwidth that your mind can afford, you start to wonder.

One evening, after you have put Zoe to sleep and Silas is taking a shower, you hear his phone buzz. You glance at its screen sitting on the kitchen counter and see a woman's name that you don't recognize: Mary L. His phone is locked, but you know the code. Curiosity gets the best of you and you open it.

"I can still taste u in my mouth. Mmmm. Can u get away before work in the A.M.?" the text reads. Your heart stops, your head feels light, and you think you might lose your dinner.

You take a picture of his phone screen with yours, put his phone down, and go into Zoe's room. You sit in the dark, watching her sleep by the light of her nightlight. As soon as the dizziness starts to wear off, tears start rolling down your cheeks.

Silas gets out of the shower, and a few minutes later you hear him call out from the kitchen: "Hey hon, I have an early meeting tomorrow . . . will need to be out of here before you get up."

Your new reality hits you like a sledgehammer: Silas, like 25 percent of married men, has been cheating on you.[1]

You call in sick the next day, unable to focus on work. Throughout the course of the day, in the solitude of your empty house, your emotions run wild. You cry with grief, you rage with anger, you blame yourself, you blame Silas, you blame Mary. By the time you have to pick Zoe up from preschool, you just feel numb.

You wait two more days before you decide to confront Silas. You wait until Zoe is asleep and then sit him down. When you show him the image of the text you intercepted, he pauses for a long minute, but doesn't try to deny it.

Silas breaks down crying. He says he hates himself for what he's done and that Mary means nothing to him. He tells you that she pursued him and that it had been so long since he felt wanted. The implication that this is your fault for not "wanting him" enough, when you're treading water just to make it through the day, makes you even more livid.

You insist that Silas tell you all of the sordid details, but he mostly manages not to. You know that hearing about it would only make it worse, but you can't stop your imagination from going wild. It sickens you. After hours of crying, screaming, talking, and crying some more, you ask Silas to stay away for a while, while you sort out your feelings. You don't know anything anymore, but you know that you need some space.

• • •

Silas starts staying with his brother and coming by on weekends to spend a little time with Zoe while you take a hot yoga class. Your aunt Ashley comes to town for a couple of months to stay with you to give you emotional and logistical support.

You and Silas find a counselor and go to her on Tuesday afternoons—both of you sneaking out of work to make your appointments. In the counseling, Silas confides further about how he hasn't felt that there was a place or a need for him in your relationship since you are so busy with work and Zoe. And your counselor helps you to find space to hear this, while also sharing your own feelings of resentment and betrayal.

Silas swears that he has ended things with Mary. You want to believe him, but the doubt lingers. One night, after a couple of glasses of Shiraz with Ashley and your close friend Frana (whose husband, coincidentally, had an affair two years ago), you look up the screenshot of the text from Mary that you still haven't discarded. Her phone number is shown on it, and you decide to give the little hussy a call.

"This is Silas's wife," you say. Silence. "Are you still sleeping with him?" After another moment of silence, the shaky voice on the other end says, "No. No, he ended it. I don't want anything more to do with your fucked-up marriage." She hangs up. Your heart is pounding from that brief interaction, but her answer is what you wanted to hear.

You always imagined that your decision would be crystal clear if your husband ever cheated on you. The marriage would be over, obviously. But now that you're in the thick of it and have had several months to process what happened and work through the array of emotions with Silas, the decision seems anything but obvious. You are not alone in this shift of ideas. While 62 percent of couples polled said they would leave their spouse if they had an affair, in reality, 70 percent stay together after an affair is revealed.[2]

You have started believing Silas that he is truly regretful and wants to make things right. You have also started owning your own role in what has gone down: it's true that you haven't been showing Silas any affection or appreciation for a long while. You have reasons for that—namely your completely over-capacity lifestyle—but you are starting to take responsibility for your part of the outcome.

Pragmatically, you want Zoe to be able to grow up with two parents and you don't want to share custody of her.

At the same time, you don't know if you can ever fully trust Silas again. One study found that people who cheated on their partner were three times more likely to cheat again.[3] And at the end of the day, the same feelings that made you feel distant toward Silas before this all went down are still there.

If you decide that you just can't forgive Silas or trust him again, and you want to end your marriage, go to Chapter 49.

If you decide to forgive Silas, keep going to counseling, and reinvest in your relationship, go to Chapter 38.

37

REPAIR OR DIVORCE

You walk back into the office nonconspicuously and sit down at your desk, trying to look like nothing happened, although you're pretty sure you look flushed. You're just coming back from a lunchtime make-out session in Jonathan's car—the third one this week.

You try to focus on your work, but ever since your flirtation with Jonathan stepped over into the physical realm a few months ago, you just haven't been able to concentrate. At first it was a fun and exciting lack of focus, but lately, you've been feeling more angsty when you are not around him. A combination of craving, guilt, and insecurity.

You picture him when you close your eyes, in scattered flashes of flesh and replayed conversations. You worry that he doesn't want you anymore, even when he was just grabbing at your blouse, his lips on your neck, only hours ago. Sometimes you loathe yourself for who you have become, but you also feel more vibrantly desirable than you ever have. It's an all-consuming whirlwind of emotions.

• • •

A few more months of this, and you start to feel the things you care most about slipping away from you. You look back at the last six months and realize that you have barely been present with Zoe, you have stopped feeling connected to Silas, and your work is suffering. This prolonged rendezvous with Jonathan has been exhilarating and has thoroughly knocked you on your ass. Now you realize you have to end it.

You tell Jonathan you can't do this anymore. He says he understands and you both embrace, whisper a few sweet nothings about how amazing this has been, and kiss goodbye.

That goodbye lasts about seven hours. He texts you saying that he misses you and you cave. You meet early the next morning before work and have a passionate reunification fling.

You beat yourself up for failing so quickly at your attempt to end things with Jonathan. You try again and make it two days this time. The next attempt lasts three days. And then one day again. This isn't working. You turn to your old friend Google for help.

You comb through articles and blog posts about ending affairs. You find an online forum full of other crazed women trying to end their unhealthy infidelities. Through this research, you emerge with a plan.

You block Jonathan's phone number and set up an auto-delete email rule. You send him one last note letting him know this is for real now. And you decide, with a large knot in your stomach, that the only way to truly hold yourself accountable and repair what you have done is to come clean to Silas.

One night after Zoe is asleep, you tell him you need to talk. You start off slowly and awkwardly, but soon you are spilling it all, crying hysterically in a fit of shame and relief. You hadn't realized how much this had all been weighing you.

For the first few days, Silas barely reacts. He just basically ignores you, with a pained expression in his hazel eyes. Then you answer his phone call in the middle of the workday, and he starts laying into you. Hard. You know you deserve this and are slightly relieved that he's finally saying something. But the words he says are so hurtful, you start to feel angry right back at him. You both say too many things to take back, and you end up having to leave work puffy-eyed and panicked.

Two days after that, Silas decides to go stay with his brother for a while, to think about what comes next. He'll come to spend a few hours visiting Zoe on the weekends. This means you have single parent responsibilities during the week. But since you are the one that brought this situation on, you make it work.

You honestly don't know what you want the outcome of this limbo to be. The distance between you and Silas was what opened you up to fall for Jonathan, and it's been a long time since you can remember feeling close to Silas. Were you ever truly close? Your heart still aches for Jonathan, even though you've finally been successful in breaking contact with him. And the words Silas said to you in his fit of anger are sticking to you in a way you can't seem to shake off.

Through your infidelity research project, you know that infidelity is the second-most cited reason for divorce, being listed as a reason by at least one partner in 88 percent of couples surveyed.[1]

In one sense, you want to be like the 70 percent of couples who make it through their marriage after infidelity.[2] You want Zoe to grow up in a two-parent household. You don't want to share custody of her. And ultimately, you don't want to be divorced.

At the same time, you wonder if Silas is really the one for you. Looking back, your status as co-parents happened by accident—even though you would never think of Zoe as accidental, as she is the best part of your life. Your marriage was a result of circumstance rather than romance. This history doesn't bode well for your future together, as couples who were married before conceiving kids have a 70 percent better chance of staying together than those who had kids first.[3]

After staying away for about a month, Silas asks you to meet up and talk. Over a cup of coffee on neutral ground, you look at each other with pain in your eyes. He says he would be willing to do the work to repair, but only if you really want that. If you really want him.

If you decide to do the hard work to rebuild your marriage, go to Chapter 47.

If you decide that your marriage is past the point of return, and you are not meant to live your life with Silas, go to Chapter 49.

38

HAPPILY EVER AFTER
WITH BATTLE SCARS

Since you started making an intentional effort to invest in your relationship with Silas, something fascinating has happened: you've actually started enjoying having him in your life again. You hadn't realized how much you had disconnected since Zoe was born, but in contrast to the work you are doing now, you see now just how far you had drifted from him.

You and Silas are seeing a couple's counselor every other week to work on your communication skills with each other and to work through logistical issues as they come up. You find that having that third party to guide you through some of the more contentious topics helps a lot.

You have also scheduled Silas's mother to come babysit so you can have a date night every other weekend. It's a little far for her, so she needs to spend the night at your small apartment on those evenings, which makes for a crowded Sunday morning. But it's much more affordable than hiring a babysitter, and she loves spending time with her granddaughter.

You have even started following through on a regularly scheduled Wednesday night sex night. Although the idea of having an amorous appointment on your calendar feels far from romantic, you find that it keeps your relationship intimate. Once you get going, it's almost as hot as spontaneous lovemaking.

You and Silas still go through phases where you question if you were meant to be together. You fight, you resent him, you wish he were different. But you also have many times over the years where you feel closer to him than anyone. You feel the kind of intimate love for him that comes from knowing someone deeply, from knowing the ugly and the beautiful sides of them, and from making it through the rough times with some bruises and scrapes, but with the strength of perseverance.

You also have the times together where Zoe does something new and amazing, from her first book report to her first time behind the wheel, and you glance at each other with a look of wonder that only one parent can give the other. These moments make the work you have done to stay together feel worth it.

And so you and Silas push through the bumpy road of life together, happily ever after with battle scars.

The End

*(Want to see what would have happened if you had decided to lean into your career more and hired a nanny to help with the childcare? Turn back to **Chapter 18** and make a different choice. Or if you've explored all the paths, turn to the **Epilogue**.)*

39

RETURNSHIP OR CRAFTSMANSHIP

You and Nathan decide to stay off of birth control and try for a second child. Since it took a couple of years to conceive Paxton, you figure the kids will be about four years apart this way. So you are quite surprised to find yourself pregnant without even having gotten your period back. This is not uncommon; many times a woman's first ovulation post-pregnancy comes before her first period, so many women find themselves surprised to be fertile, let alone pregnant, in such a short time period.[1]

Your pregnancy goes smoothly, although you find it much more exhausting this time around. This may be partially due to you being only a year out from the last time your body got hijacked by a growing human, Paxton, who is still feeding off of you, and it may be partially because you have to simultaneously take care of Paxton, work full-time, and gestate. The concept of "me time" isn't part of your vocabulary anymore.

One spring evening, you and Nathan leave Paxton with your visiting mother and head to the hospital when your contractions are four minutes apart. This delivery goes quickly, and by morning, you have a beautiful baby girl in your arms. You name her Fiona.

During your maternity leave, you do a lot of soul searching. With two children under two and the high cost of daycare, you will be spending more than you make if you go back to work. You also really want to be with your babies while they are still babies. Although you do enjoy your job, you don't feel that it defines you.

You decide to stay home with your kids for a couple of years, at least until they are both in preschool. Nathan is supportive of this decision. Finances will be a little tight with you not working, but no tighter than they would have been with childcare expenses.

The first twenty-one months of Paxton's life, up until Fiona was born, read like a brochure published by the American Society of Pediatrics. He was exclusively breastfed, he started organic baby food at six months, and he didn't lay eyes on a single screen. You made sure that a creak wasn't made in the house when he was sleeping, and that everyone who came around him had washed their hands and gotten vaccinated.

Given this, you imagine that Paxton must be a bit surprised and entertained by the sudden shift in regulations once his sister is in the picture. The energy it took to maintain a textbook healthy childhood is suddenly not available anymore. You start letting Paxton watch *Elmo,* give him Ritz crackers between meals, and bring both children along for the ride when you have an errand to run or an appointment to keep. Naptime be damned.

You think to yourself often how you wish you had known how easy it was to care for one child, back when you only had one. Ensuring that two kids are safe, happy, and healthy is about six times more challenging than with just one. But you still enjoy the chaos and cuteness and are glad that you made the choice to be present for these years.

You also start getting very creative with enriching activities to keep the kids entertained as they transition from babyhood to toddler years. In addition to plenty of time on the playground and at the children's museum, you convert your dining nook to a craft center and curate a seemingly never-ending array of art projects. From Play-doh to finger paints to paper mâché: you are practically running a child art gallery incubator.

One afternoon, as the children beg to go outside to play and you push them to just paint a little longer, "so mommy can finish up her artwork," you realize that the craft corner is more for you than them. You never really saw yourself as crafty before, but you've come to feel an insatiable urge to create. It's kind of fun.

• • •

As Fiona nears three years old and Paxton gets ready to enroll in kindergarten, you find yourself planning for some spare time on the horizon. You and Nathan talk about the options ahead of you.

When you decided to quit your job to stay home with the kids, you had fully planned to get back into the workforce at about this time. Now that you have gotten into the routine of stay-at-home motherhood and have worked your way through the boredom and self-doubt into a state of fulfillment, you feel slightly less sure of that plan.

You always enjoyed working before. And now that Paxton is entering kindergarten at your local public school, the finances will work out in your favor if you get back to the salary you had. You imagine it won't be too difficult to find another job as a copy editor—maybe not in people management again right away, but you figure you can move back up to that. You have a hunch that being employed will be good for your confidence too, since you still feel a tinge self-conscious when people ask you what you do. Many are in this same boat: of women who took time off from their career, 93 percent want to return. Of these, 46 percent want to do so primarily for the independent income, and 43 percent for the "enjoyment and satisfaction."[2]

The biggest reason that you are considering not going back is one that you didn't expect. It's the arts and crafts. Now that you have discovered this creative outlet, and because the work you are producing is not half-bad, you find yourself wanting to invest more time into this passion. If you suddenly have time to yourself during the day, you can see yourself setting up a little art studio and delving into this endeavor further. So far, your favorite medium is watercolor painting, but that's been limited by the materials that you've allowed around the children. You'd love to explore some more toxic and costly mediums as well.

If you choose to rejoin the corporate workforce in order to increase your family's budget and your sense of professional worth, go to Chapter 53.

If you decide to pursue your creative passions instead of returning to work, go to Chapter 51.

40

PAY IT BACK OR FORWARD

You found a meaningful job that you mostly enjoy as a project manager for the philanthropic arm of a large enterprise software company. You are using much of the knowledge that you acquired in your master's program and are working on some challenging and interesting projects. Even though the balance between work and being a single mother feels taxing at times, you have a strong community of friends supporting you.

While Lily is in daycare and preschool, you barely make ends meet. But even though your rent payment almost gives you ulcers each month, and your family members don't receive gifts from you for several years, you manage to survive this chapter. The day that Lily starts kindergarten and your daycare expenses finally come to an end, you feel as though you just received a 25 percent raise. You finally feel like you can breathe again.

This newfound "raise" has a clear destination: the student loans that you have been mostly kicking down the road over the past five years. Even though one in four American adults are paying off student loans with an average of $37,000 borrowed, and 60 percent of borrowers expect to pay off their loans in their forties, you feel a self-conscious weight on your shoulders.[1] You are in your thirties now and feel like you should be saving for Lily's education and your retirement, rather than endlessly paying down your debt.

Apparently, many of your new coworker friends don't have this same issue. As you become closer to them, you start getting invited to charity galas, auctions, and luncheons—each with a minimum suggested donation. This seems to be a significant part of the social life of this new crowd you find yourself in, and you're not sure you can keep up.

Everyone appears to have a cause that they are passionate about, which they volunteer for and donate money to. You admire their generosity and passion, and long to do the same. You just wonder how you can afford to be a single mother with hefty student loans, while still giving back to your community. You know that 25 percent of American adults volunteer their time and about half donate money averaging about $2,500 a year.[2]

One day, as you are driving Lily to school, she asks you why the man on the side of the road is holding a sign that says, "need help." Your first emotion is pride that she read the sign, followed quickly by guilt and despair about the social inequalities that surround you and doubt over how to explain these to your innocent daughter. You want to lead by example and inspire her to make the world a better place as she grows up.

Part of you wants to invest your small amount of extra money into paying off your student debt and saving for your and Lily's futures. The burden of loans weighs heavy on you and your safety net is weak at best.

At the same time, you want to give back to your community, as there are many people worse off than you are. You would love to invest your spare money and time into causes

that help others. You want to inspire Lily with generosity—
and getting to take part in the celebrations of giving that your
peers invite you to wouldn't be a bad side effect either.

*If you decide to pay back your student loans faster so that you
can save for your future, go to **Chapter 50**.*

*If you decide to keep paying the minimum on your loans so
that you can pay your good fortune forward and start a charitable giving plan, go to **Chapter 57**.*

41

YOUR HOME OR A CARE HOME

You pick Paxton up from preschool and stop off at the grocery store to grab a rotisserie chicken for dinner. "We're going to visit Grandma this weekend," you tell him. Paxton squeals with delight—he's had a close relationship with your mother since he was a baby and she moved to Eugene to be closer to you. Unfortunately, you haven't stayed as close to your father since their divorce, as he remarried and remained across the country; Paxton has only seen him a handful of times. But having your mother only a two-hour drive away has been meaningful for all of you.

That Saturday, you, Nathan, and Paxton pile into your Volvo station wagon and drive down to visit your mom, as you do every couple of months. You arrive and unload the bags for your overnight stay as Paxton runs into her arms, almost knocking her over. You look past him into the house and notice a lot of clutter. This is surprising, as your mother is known for her immaculate housekeeping. You come in and start to tidy up.

Over dinner that evening, you mention that it might be helpful to get someone to come in and help with cleaning every now and then. After all, she is nearing seventy and could probably use some extra help with the house. Her reaction takes you off guard: she yells that she doesn't need any help, slams her glass down, and walks out of the room. Paxton and Nathan both look at you in surprise, and you get up to check on her.

You find her standing in the laundry room, looking lost. You give her a hug and bring her up to her bedroom. She doesn't say much, and everyone settles down for the evening.

The next day brings two more unexpected outbursts from your mother. She has always been such a calm and steady force in your life, so this is unsettling. She just doesn't seem like herself.

You call your brother, Jonas when you get back home and tell him about what you observed. He decides that he is due for a visit anyway, so he makes plans to fly into town in a few weeks, and the two of you plan to go for a maternal visit together.

The visit with your brother reinforces your worries: your mother's house is in a state of disarray and she seems confused and irritable. After a weekend of observation and reflection, and some panic-inducing internet searches, you and Jonas decide you need to take your mother to the doctor. The doctor confirms your fears: your mother is showing early signs of dementia.

Although your mother is far from alone in this diagnosis—over 50 million people are living with dementia worldwide—the fear and heartbreak that you all feel are severe.[1] The doctor tells you what you have already started to understand: your mother can no longer safely live by herself.

You and Jonas make the drive back to your house to discuss options with Nathan. Jonas is living with his family in Austin, and you all agree that relocating your mother there isn't an option, as he wouldn't have the flexibility to care for her, and the climate difference could be hard for her. Although you could get a caregiver to come live in her house, you still don't feel comfortable being that far away from her as her condition worsens. It looks like the most viable options are to move her into an assisted living facility near you or convert your basement into living quarters for her.

You visit a few local assisted living places to get a feel for what options are out there. Although there are some nice ones, and some that are specifically geared toward memory care for dementia patients, which are, of course, more expensive, they all have kind of a sterile, cold feel. The thought of putting her in a "home" makes you all feel sad. You know she wouldn't want to be there, and you want her to be surrounded by people who love her. The price is also high for these care facilities; even the cheapest is higher than your mortgage![2] Your mother could likely pay for this with her savings and by selling her house, but doing so will likely end up draining her finances.

There is also a high upfront cost for converting your basement into a living space for your mom. It is already partially finished, but you would need to put a bathroom down there, make some of the space more accessible for her, and generally freshen it up. You would also lose Paxton's playroom to this conversion.

Even if your mother lives with you, you will still need to hire a caregiver to come help out at some point, since you and Nathan both work. And you worry about the impact this will have on Paxton—seeing his grandma deteriorate right in front of him. Not to mention that your small house already feels a little cramped sometimes with just the three of you. About one-third of the adult population in the US lives in a "shared" household with other non-spousal adults, and 14 percent of those are the aging parent of the household head (this number has doubled in the past twenty years), so you would be in good company housing your mother.[3] Not that solidarity makes the situation any easier.

You need to make a decision quickly, as every day that your mother is living alone has you worried. Nathan tells you that he is supportive of either choice, although you know that he values his space and privacy, and Jonas is willing to help get her settled and share expenses that come up.

If you decide to convert your basement to a place for your mother to live and take on caring for her as her dementia progresses, go to Chapter 45.

If you decide that there just isn't room in your small house for another person and you will find a caring assistance facility for your mother, go to Chapter 48.

42

HAPPILY EVER AFTER CHANGING COURSE

You and Forrest continue with your wedding plans, having settled on sharing his name. You can tell that the stress from the myriad of life changes all at once is getting to him, as his emotions erupt over seemingly nothing a few times. But he is always apologetic and communicative afterward, so you brush it under the rug.

The week before your wedding, however, his outburst has you concerned. He asks if you invited his mother's bridge club, and you tell him that you didn't even know about them. He gets furious and storms out of your apartment. You start to question if you're doing something wrong to trigger this. You don't think so, but you love Forrest and trust that if he is so angry, there must be a reason. Your logic and your emotions are at odds with each other, and the result is pure confusion.

It is in this state of confusion that you push down some nagging doubts and proceed with the wedding. You don't want to admit your concerns to anyone, so you go forward like nothing is wrong.

You have a lovely ceremony and a blissed-out honeymoon phase, and you convince yourself that it was all nerves that were making Forrest act so strangely before you got married. He is still the man you fell in love with.

Your writing career is going well and you feel like you're starting to make a name for yourself. Even though you officially changed your name after the wedding, you haven't changed your byline in the paper or on your blog. One day, Forrest brings this up, and you brush the topic off as something you'll think about later. He explodes and accuses you of not being fully committed to him. This reaction makes you less interested in taking his name and brings up the feelings of anxiety that you experienced before the wedding.

You confide in a few close girlfriends about Forrest's unpredictable reactions, and they all agree it is something you should get ahead of. They suggest going to counseling with him, and you think that's a good idea. But when you bring up the idea of counseling with Forrest, he only gets angrier. He thinks couples' therapy is the beginning of the end and feels hurt that you would suggest it.

You've only been married to Forrest for a year and together for two years, but you're not feeling optimistic about your relationship at this point. Every time you try to bring up his behavior or ideas for working through it together, he only gets more erratic.

You are sad and scared, and you feel like a failure. The man that you decided you wanted to spend your life with is turning out to be a plague on your happiness and mental stability. Since Forrest won't go to counseling with you, you decide to go alone. And what you uncover, through therapy and the support of some close friends, is that you need to leave Forrest before his verbal explosions evolve into something much more dangerous for you.

Not surprisingly, Forrest takes this decision terribly. You knew he would, so you have already lined up a place to stay at your friend Celeste's house, along with her three-year-old son and two dogs.

The next six months feel like some of the worst of your life, as you go through moving out, getting divorced, and communicating to everyone who had just been at your wedding a year ago. But you also recognize how lucky you are to have friends who can support you, that you have your own financial means to recover, and that you don't need to worry about children like many women who leave abusive partners.[1] You are also privileged to not have to be afraid of law enforcement or of reinforcing stereotypes when leaving an abusive situation, which is an additional hurdle that women of color face.[2]

Getting back on your feet isn't easy. You have to get a full-time job as a copywriter in order to receive the health insurance that you had been relying on Forrest for, find a new apartment that you can afford on your own, and continue going to extensive therapy.

But you survive this and are stronger because of it. You now know the warning signs of an unhealthy relationship and you trust in yourself to do the right thing in future relationships. Moved by what you have just endured, you start volunteering at an abuse hotline to try to help other women in similar situations. You live happily ever after, even after marrying the wrong person, having changed course.

The End

(Want to see what would have happened if you had decided not to take Forrest's name? Turn back to Chapter 33 and make a different choice. Or if you've explored all the paths, turn to the Epilogue.)

43

MULTIGENERATIONAL HAPPILY EVER AFTER

When you first move back to your hometown, you move back in with your mother. Living with her feels like taking about twenty steps back in life, but it's not all that uncommon, as 15 percent of twenty-five- to thirty-year-olds live with their parents.[1] Multigenerational living arrangements are even higher for Asian, Black, and Hispanic families in the US.[2]

Aside from the complex it gives you, it's actually kind of nice being around her. Before you had Lily, she used to fall into the lovable-but-somewhat-annoying category for you. But having a daughter of your own has made you appreciate all that she did for you as a child and also all that she is doing for you now, especially helping out with Lily. You even have some special bonding girlfriend moments over a bottle of wine in the evenings.

That's why, when a small two-bedroom house becomes available for rent down the block, you decide to take it. Being close to your mother long-term sounds comforting to you.

You've found a job as the director of the local community center; it's not the dream job you had in mind while you were in your master's program, but it pays the bills and it feels good to be well connected to your community. The community center even has a preschool, which you're able to enroll Lily in. It's nice being close to her during the day.

Lily and your mother form a very close relationship. This is a lot of fun for both of them, and it allows you a little alone time here and there, during which you start writing a book of poetry. The resounding theme in your writing is the beauty and symmetry in the generational cycles of life, inspired by the three generations of women that you have brought together.

When your mother unexpectedly passes away a few years later, you are forever grateful that you had this time for the three of you to be close. The help that she gave you when you were just starting out as a single mother, and the relationship that she built with your daughter, will forever be with you. You will grieve her loss forever, but you live happily ever after with the imprint of that multigenerational bond.

The End

(Want to see what would have happened if you had decided not to move back to your hometown? Turn back to Chapter 24 and make a different choice. Or if you've explored all the paths, turn to the Epilogue.)

44

PRESCRIBE OR MANAGE

You pull off your sneakers in the elevator and swap them out for the three-inch patent leather heels in your bag. As you walk into the office, you grab a stack of notes from your assistant, Abby, and hand her your outerwear as you hurry into your first meeting. Since turning up your professional game, you have had two promotions in as many years and are now managing the global corporate social responsibility program for your company. Although this sounds glamorous, it actually involves a lot of putting out fires and negotiating for resources. But you find that you're pretty adept, if not outright good, at it.

Around four in the afternoon, you get a text from your nanny, Faith, with a picture of Zoe swinging on the zip line after school. You smile at her bravery and feel a brief moment of wistfulness as you long to be there with her. But you push that feeling back and jump onto a conference call with the San Francisco office.

You lie in bed that night, unable to fall asleep again. The conversations you had that day keep playing through your head: Did you say the wrong thing to Ted? Did Shelly know you were only joking when you heckled her about her project? Does Abby think you're too demanding?

You started noticing this second-guessing in yourself around the time that you started making a conscious effort to be "more professional" at work. By filtering your words so you only use those that you think people want to hear, you find yourself always wondering if you did, in fact, apply the right filter. It's gotten worse since your last promotion, as you find yourself in rooms with top decision-makers who all seem to be more in their element than you. Do they think you're faking it?

You also have a never-ending to-do list running through your head. The work portion of it includes all of the people you need to follow up with, the articles you need to read, the projects you need to get going on, and the emails you need to reply to. The home portion includes scheduling gymnastics lessons, play dates, and a doctor's appointment for Zoe, and going through her clothes to see what actually still fits her after her recent growth spurt. None of these items should be keeping you up at night, but the combination of them has your head spinning.

You finally fall asleep around 1:00 A.M., only to wake up again at 4:00 A.M. with a feeling of dread that you can't pinpoint. During the day, you feel an underlying sense of exhaustion and confusion from not having slept well for more nights than you can count. You check your email to see if Simon replied to your last note—did you come across as too pushy?

• • •

One Wednesday morning, in the middle of a weekly update meeting, you feel your heart start to pound out of your chest, you break into a sweat, and you feel like you can't breathe. You think something must be seriously wrong with you and you run out of the room and into the elevator. From the downstairs lobby, you call Silas and ask him to come get you—you think you might have had a heart attack or something.

At the ER, you check out just fine and they send you home. A week later, when you have another similar occurrence, you make an appointment with your primary care doctor. She says it sounds like you've been having panic attacks and recommends that you see a psychiatrist. At first, you don't believe her; your symptoms were purely physical, not mental. But upon further research and after a trip to the psychiatrist she referred you to, Dr. Malone, you reluctantly accept the diagnosis.

Dr. Malone says that you have an anxiety disorder. Not only does this explain the panic attacks you've had recently, but it also accounts for your sleepless nights and obsessive thoughts. He suggests medication. You hate the thought of being medicated long-term; you've always been wary of Big Pharma, and you like to believe that you can handle your issues yourself without the help of drugs. You feel alone and ashamed for being in this state to begin with, even though 18 percent of adults in the US suffer from an anxiety disorder, and 37 percent of those receive treatment.[1]

You talk it over with Silas, and he is supportive of you going on medication. He's noticed the difference in you over the past year or so and he wants the old you back. At first you feel offended by this; it seems as if he's not on your side. But after thinking it over more, you can kind of understand where he is coming from. If you're being honest with yourself, you haven't really felt the same as you used to, and you miss feeling more in the moment and relaxed.

You can't help but feel like you'd be giving in and showing weakness by depending on drugs for your mental state, though. You don't want to build your life on a false foundation of medication. You feel torn over what to do, and that is making you feel even more anxious.

If you decide to go on antianxiety medication, go to Chapter 55.

If you decide to manage on your own without medication, go to Chapter 56.

45

SANDWICHED

Your basement remodel is completed with sadly uncanny timing. The same day you do the final walkthrough with the contractors, you get a call from the temporary caregiver you hired to look after your mom in her house. She has fallen getting into the shower and is in the hospital. You rush down there and find out that she has broken her hip.

This makes her move into your new guest suite even more urgent. She is discharged from the hospital directly into your home. You hadn't planned for this to happen quite so soon, and you haven't lined up a new daytime caregiver for her yet. You have to take two weeks off to get her moved and to be with her during the day until you find someone. You also need to quickly swap out the queen guest bed for a hospital bed.

You hire a realtor to put your mom's house on the market, and Jonas comes back to help pack her things. Although she already thinned out many of her belongings before moving cross-country several years ago, you still need to store or purge many mementos. Your sentimental side triumphs and you end up with boxes of old volleyball trophies and year-books in your garage.

• • •

Even after you hire a daytime caregiver, close on the sale of your mom's house, and get into a routine again, your life is far from relaxed. Every time you think you're managing, a new curveball comes your way. One day you find your mother digging up all of the plants in your front planting strip. The next day she throws a fit about the dinner you made her, saying that it is disgusting (even though she has always liked your lasagna). Meanwhile, you see Paxton getting more afraid of interacting with her, which breaks your heart.

You finally have to have a talk with your manager to explain the circumstances at home. Even with a paid daytime caregiver, you find yourself being late for work and getting called home in the middle of the day for emergencies. You didn't realize just how much time this arrangement would require of you. Like 43.5 million Americans who provide unpaid care for an older adult, you find yourself spending over 20 hours a week on caregiving tasks.[1] Fortunately, your manager is understanding, as she herself has had to help with an aging parent before, and she gives you the flexibility you need.

One day you get a call from Paxton's school rather than the more expected caregiver's call; Paxton threw up and needs to go home. This is such a normal occurrence for a parent, but the timing of it almost breaks you. You cry the entire drive to the school. This overwhelmed feeling is a clear symptom of being part of the *sandwich generation*—adults who are caring both for their children and their parents. Of middle-aged Americans, 15 percent are providing financial support to both their parents and their children, and 38 percent are providing emotional support to both.[2]

The pain of being pulled in two directions this way is almost physical.

. . .

Over time, your mother's condition worsens. She can no longer move around on her own, she barely remembers who you are, and she has no recollection of Nathan or Paxton. She also frequently asks for your father, who she divorced almost twenty years ago. You feel so much sadness and stress over seeing her this way and having to do the hard work of taking care of her. You start to resent Jonas for not being around to help even though he checks in frequently and shares expenses. This is a dark time for you.

Then your mother gets sick. It starts with a cold but progresses to pneumonia. She spends two weeks in the hospital, and the doctor finally suggests that you have her loved ones come and visit her.

You take a leave of absence from work. After calling Jonas, your Aunt Ashley, and several of your mother's close friends to come to pay their respects, you hunker down by your mother's side in the hospital.

As you do, you go to Chapter 52.

46

EXPLORE OTHER OPTIONS

You thank Michael for the feedback and tell him you will work on your executive presence. But in reality, you don't really try to change who you are. You keep doing great work and carrying yourself professionally, hoping that will be enough to grow your career there.

Your friend Anna, who you have been tight with since you were in grad school, is going through a somewhat similar situation at her work. After her son was diagnosed with autism, as about one in fifty-nine children in the US are, she has had to take time off in the afternoons for his appointments.[1] She has been staying on top of her work and is convinced that she hasn't dropped the ball on a single assignment. But she confides in you that she is being criticized by her manager for lack of face time.

Between your experience and Anna's, in which you are both doing great work but are being held back because of perceptions, you feel a building resentment toward corporate norms.

After two more review periods consisting of positive performance feedback, squishy personality feedback, and no promotions, you decide it's probably time to see what else is out there.

As you do, you continue on to Chapter 58.

47

HAPPILY EVER AFTER HAVING TRIED YOUR BEST

Knowing that the longevity of your marriage depends on you fixing both yourself and your relationship, you have started going to individual and couples counseling sessions. This means that you are in therapy twice a week, which is a major commitment of time and emotional energy. But you know this is necessary if you're going to rebuild.

In your individual sessions, you start to examine the void you had been trying to fill with your relationship with Jonathan and think through healthier ways to fill it in the future. You also explore your relationship issues as they relate to your parents' dysfunctional marriage. You learn about your triggers and get new vocabulary to better communicate your feelings.

In your couples counseling, you do equal parts talking and listening. Silas feels betrayed, and you need to give him the space to talk through his feelings. While repenting for your role in that, you also have a lot of valid needs that haven't been met. Your counselor is good and helps you both hear each other.

As you go further down the road to repair your marriage and have your head more fully out of the cloud of your affair, you start to feel more guilty and almost repulsed by what you let happen with Jonathan. The fact that he was able to get you in a tailspin over a little flirty attention makes you feel ashamed of your weakness. You resolve never to be that weak or susceptible again.

With all of the work you are doing and revelations you are having, you start to feel more optimistic than you have in a long time that you can get through this with your marriage intact. The odds are in your favor: In marriages where infidelity was confessed, almost 60 percent stay married (as opposed to 20 percent when the infidelity stayed a secret).[1]

Your therapy sessions continue but become a bit less frequent as you build up your relationship tools and progress into maintenance mode. You and Silas discover a new way of being together. You are both humbled by what you have been through and determined to make it work going forward.

And you do make it work, for several more years. You share some beautiful times together as a family of three. But even though you and Silas have repaired the trust between you, and you manage to not slip into infidelity again, you never really flourish together in romantic love. Perhaps you never had that foundation to begin with.

When Zoe is eleven, you and Silas decide that you are better as co-parents than as a couple. You divorce amicably, move into apartments in the same building, and live happily ever after having tried your best.

The End

(Want to see what would have happened if you had resisted temptation with Jonathan? Turn back to Chapter 28 and make a different choice. Or if you've explored all the paths, turn to the Epilogue.)

48

GUILT COMPLEX

You pull up to Orchard Heights, the assisted living facility where your mother now lives, for your regular Sunday evening dinner with her. You have Nathan and Paxton with you, and you bring her a bouquet of lilies to replace the wilting one from last week. They are her favorite flower.

You wait in your mother's 600-square-foot apartment filled with her favorite subset of furniture and decor from her house while her caregiver helps her use the bathroom. Then the four of you head down to the dining hall for a bland meal of chicken, vegetables, and rice, all of which taste roughly the same to you. Amazingly, your mother seems happier with this food than the gourmet cooking you have been trying to push on her.

As your mother pushes her walker back to her apartment, you look around at the myriad of elders wandering the halls and sitting on couches. Some seem lucid, others, not so much. This glaring view into the downward slope near the end of life's journey makes you both sad and uncomfortable. With life expectancy from birth going up over 60 percent for white men and women and over 100 percent for black men and women over the last century, it's no wonder nursing homes like your mother's are full of elders who are barely hanging on to their vibrancy and wherewithal.[1] And with more than half of the patients in assisted living facilities having some form of dementia or cognitive impairment, the confusion and aimlessness that you observe around you are unsettling.[2] Although you are grateful for every day that you still have your mother with you, you can't help but feel mixed feelings about this trend.

You continue with these weekly dinner visits, along with occasional longer stays when you're able to break away on a weekday afternoon, for the next year. You feel a consistent nagging guilt with every encounter, thinking about how much more personal it would be to have your mother at your house. But then you also feel guilty for the sense of relief you feel over that not being the arrangement. As your mother continues to deteriorate, you see how much work it would be to take care of her yourself.

Eventually, your mother becomes so helpless that she needs to move out of her small apartment and into an assisted care room, where nurses can watch over her constantly. A few months after that, your mother's doctor tells you that her systems are shutting down. After drilling the doctor with hypothetical questions and talking it over with Jonas, you decide it is time to place her on hospice. You invite your mother's relatives and old friends to come pay their last respects. As you do, you continue on to *Chapter 52*.

49

HAPPILY EVER AFTER SHARING CUSTODY

Silas has found an apartment about a mile away from you and has moved out. The process of watching him pack all of his belongings and empty your small apartment, one carload after another, is heartbreaking. Having to tell your parents that your marriage is ending is even worse. You feel ashamed around the other kindergarten parents, imagining that they all know the sordid details of your failed marriage. This feels like a low point in your life.

For several months you don't initiate a divorce, and Silas doesn't bring it up. You are in survival mode, and legal proceedings feel like more than you can stomach. Maybe there is also a small part of you that hopes for a miracle in terms of salvaging your marriage, but that glimmer of hope is waning by the day.

Silas comes by to visit with Zoe on weekends, and you get out of the apartment while he's there. Your life as Zoe's primary caregiver, and your need to vacate your apartment during peak relaxation times, finally gives you the push you need to make your divorce and custody plan official.

You and Silas don't have too much in terms of shared assets since you have both been paying off student loans. You are amicable to dividing the small savings that you do have evenly, which simplifies the legal legwork. That means that a shared custody plan for Zoe is the biggest item to figure out.

You and Silas decide to try to come to a custody agreement without the expensive help of a lawyer. Twenty-nine percent of custody decisions are made without the assistance of a court or mediator, and 91 percent of decisions are made without a ruling from a family court.[1] If they can do it, so can you!

Your heart tells you that you don't want to be away from Zoe more than you already are when you're at work. But your mind (fueled by research), tells you that the best thing for her is to have both of her parents raising her. Children who spend at least 35 percent of their time with each parent forge better relationships with both parents and do better academically, socially, and psychologically.[2] In the end, you and Silas agree to switch off every two to three days with where Zoe stays and agree to revisit the arrangement as she gets older.

The first night that Zoe sleeps at Silas's apartment is excruciating. You pace around the apartment, unsure of what to do with yourself, crying intermittently out of loneliness and anger. But it doesn't take all that long before you start finding solace in the time you have to yourself. You are able to read books for the first time in ages and even start doing some writing of your own. It's nice to have the flexibility to go out with friends sometimes or even start going out on dates after a while.

As Zoe grows up, you adjust the custody arrangement to the needs of her schedule and your work schedules. Your relationship with your ex-husband is never a solid friendship, but as time goes on, you are able to manage things warmly and productively, and you both are able to give Zoe the support and love she needs to thrive.

You eventually find your new normal, enjoy the balance of time with Zoe and time alone, and live happily ever after sharing custody.

The End

*(Want to see what would have happened if you had tried to repair your marriage instead? Turn back to **Chapter 37** and make a different choice. Or if you've explored all the paths, turn to the **Epilogue**.)*

50

AN ILLUSTRATED
HAPPILY EVER AFTER

You put yourself on a rigid monthly budget: tracking each purchase, eating out no more than once a month, and paying back your student loans at double the minimum amount. You calculate that you'll be able to save $6,000 in interest through this increased repayment schedule, which you plan to put towards Lily's college savings. Although you're not living lavishly, this plan has you feeling more in control and on top of your financial fate.

One night, after Lily goes to sleep, you decide to surprise her with a cute little drawing of the day you had together at the playground. You draw it in comic format, showing a little girl named Lily swinging higher and sliding faster than anyone ever has before. You show it to her the next morning and she squeals with delight. Inspired by her reaction, you draw another similar comic about Lily's adventures in preschool the next week. You get a similar reaction from her of joy and pride. You realize that you love both the process of drawing these comics for her and her reaction to them.

Since you're not keeping much of an active social life—with your limited restaurant budget and your need to turn down all the charity events—after Lily goes to bed, you start spending your evenings drawing a series of "Super Lily" comics.

You show the comics to your brother when he is in town for a visit. They're mostly just piled up on your dining room table, with a few favorites hanging in Lily's room. He tells you that they're actually really good and that you should start sharing them.

Inspired by his words of encouragement, you photograph all of the comics and start posting them on Instagram under the new identity of Super Lily. To your surprise, you start getting quite a few followers. You make some Super Lily t-shirts and stickers and end up selling about $100 a month of them. It's definitely nothing to quit your day job over, but you enjoy this new creative outlet and small fanbase.

With your Super Lily money, you take Lily out for pizza and ice-cream sundaes to celebrate. It's over this ice-cream date that Lily tells you that she wants to be just like you when she grows up. You know these are the love-struck words of a five-year-old, but they mean the world to you.

You continue working as a project manager and creating Super Lily comics on the side. Seven years later, you make your very last student loan payment. By that time, you have already gotten a couple of raises and found a way to start giving back to your community as well. You live happily ever after illustrating the super girl you see in your daughter.

The End

(Want to see what would have happened if you had decided to pay it forward instead? Turn back to Chapter 40 and make a different choice. Or if you've explored all the paths, turn to the Epilogue.)

51

HAPPILY EVER AFTER CREATING

You have enrolled in a continuing learning painting class at the local community college. A few students are around your age, and many more are a decade or two younger, but you don't care. You love the instructor, and getting access to grown-up paint supplies made by companies other than Crayola is liberating.

You become increasingly comfortable with oil paints on canvas. When you're not in class, you often take your supplies outside and focus on painting plants and landscapes. One day, you realize you are out of canvas and only have two hours until you need to pick the kids up. You tear the side off of an Amazon box that was in the recycling bin and start to paint on that. The texture, the way it absorbs the paint, the "recycled" look of it . . . it captures you.

Next, you start exploring painting on scrap pieces of wood. Nathan and the kids start a joke about mom rummaging through the trash for her art, but you can tell they dig it. After some experimenting, you eventually converge on simple self-constructed wooden boxes that you paint with abstract nature designs. You've found your niche, and you love it.

You start selling your creations at the local farmers market, and you're able to move quite a few of them each weekend. Eventually, when Paxton and Fiona get older, they come help you at your stand. They feel proud being able to help mom out, and you love the time you get with them.

The thought of going back to corporate America still flits through your mind from time to time, but not in a wistful or regretful way. You are happy with the path you have taken, although it means making sure your family's ends are met from a single salary. With Nathan paying off both of your student loans, in addition to your monthly bills, you only get to eat out at restaurants for special occasions, and you don't have the little luxuries some of your friends have, like a house cleaner or a gym membership. But no one seems to mind too much, and you can no longer imagine living a life that didn't give you this creative outlet. And so you live happily ever after, creating.

The End

(Want to see what would have happened if you had decided to go back to work instead? Turn back to Chapter 39 and make a different choice. Or if you've explored all the paths, turn to the Epilogue.)

52

HAPPILY EVER AFTER
NEVER FORGETTING

The weeks following your mother's death pass in a blur. You have relatives and family friends coming in and out of your home bringing flowers and casseroles. You work with your brother on an obituary, but turn down the opportunity to speak at her funeral. You feel too consumed with grief and logistics to put your feelings into audible words.

One morning, while you are getting Paxton ready for school, he says to you, "Do you think Grandma would still be alive if we had done something different?" This innocent question stops you in your tracks, as it verbalizes the question you didn't realize you have been asking yourself. But as you answer your son, the truth becomes clear to you too: there is no path you could have taken that would have kept your mother from slipping away. Whether she lived with you or at an assisted living facility or even stayed in her house, she was going to go from this world when she did. This realization gives you some peace from guilt, although not from grief.

Over time, you start to find beauty in your sadness. Little things remind you of your mother: an expression on Paxton's face, lilies blooming in the spring, a favorite song of hers coming on the radio. Although you will always miss her and never fully stop grieving her loss, you find that you are able to go on. Even the pain you feel at her loss is a comfort; it's a vivid expression of how deeply you love her. It is the strength that she fortified in you that keeps you going. It is the mother that she was to you that will make you the best mother you can be for Paxton.

You live your life with memories of your mother in your heart, and you live happily ever after, never forgetting her.

The End

(Want to see what would have happened if you had decided to have two children? Turn back to **Chapter 27** *and make a different choice. Or if you've explored all the paths, turn to the* **Epilogue***.)*

53

STICK IT OUT OR BACK OUT

You start your search for a new job optimistically. You were a top performer in your last role as a marketing manager and have always had a fairly easy time finding employment. You research which companies you would most want to work for based on company culture and mission and start applying to relevant roles within those companies; you then sit back and wait for the interviews to get scheduled.

To your surprise, the recruiter calls don't start pouring in. You do get one phone screening call, in which the recruiter asks you only about the time that you took off and not the work you did before that. Two days later, you get an automated email saying that the job has been filled.

Now that you're waking up to the fact that this job search is going to be tougher than you anticipated, you decide to double down and get less picky. You start browsing job boards and applying to almost any role that looks like it matches your qualifications. Although you start out applying for management jobs—like the one that you left three years ago—you subsequently begin applying for individual contributor roles as well.

You finally start getting some in-person interviews. But even those are disheartening. You keep getting asked why you took time off, what you did during that time, and even how you expect to manage a full-time job now with your kids still so young. You have to proactively bring up your past experience and accomplishments in most of the conversations.

You realize that you're probably going to need an "in" to get your foot back in the door. You start having coffee with everyone you know who's in the corporate sector and asking each of them who else you should approach. It is through one of these second-degree connections that you hear about a job as a copywriter at a marketing agency. Lainey, the friend of a friend who gets you the interview, puts in a good word for you. They make you an offer.

• • •

Your first day back at work is daunting. Despite the fact that you're starting off two levels lower than your last job, and you have the feeling that you could do the work in your sleep, you still feel intimidated by the environment. At first you are happy to hear that your new manager is a woman named Alexis—you are looking forward to some female solidarity. Alexis, it turns out, is ten years your junior, extremely ambitious and, having no kids of her own, has very little sympathy for the balancing act of a working mother.

Your colleagues also all skew to the younger side. They go out for happy hour most nights after work—an activity that they stopped inviting you to after your first several answers of "thanks, but I have to pick up my kids." They are all fairly competitive in their work style too. You find that you need to really dig in to prove yourself—a task that feels difficult since you are still the primary caregiver for Paxton and Fiona, and as such, need to do things like pick them up when they're sick, sign them up for swim classes, and occasionally volunteer for field trips.

You are making much less money than you had anticipated you would when you decided to plunge back into the workforce. Your calculations were based on your previous salary, which was about $25,000 more than you are making now. This is unfortunate, but not surprising. Although the average time that a woman takes off from work is only 2.2 years, this results in a decrease of earning power of 18 percent, which rises to 37 percent when women take more than 3 years out of the workforce.[1]

This combination of feeling under-leveled, underpaid, and overextended starts to wear on you pretty quickly. You begin to doubt your decision to get back into the workforce and find yourself longing for simpler times of playing with kids and making crafts.

At the same time, you're enjoying the actual work you are doing. It turns out you're still damn good at it, and that feels invigorating. Although your current pay and workplace dynamics are an energy drain, you have a feeling that you can build back respect and salary by nailing your assignments.

*If you decide to back out of your decision to get back into the rat race, return to the life you had before, and pursue your creative passions instead, go to **Chapter 51**.*

*If you decide to stick it out and do the work to reestablish yourself in the corporate world, go to **Chapter 54**.*

54

HAPPILY EVER AFTER REESTABLISHED

If you could describe your first year back at work with one word, it would be *grit*. You feel like you had to work twice as hard as the rest of your colleagues just to prove yourself and twice as hard as the rest of the moms you know just to keep up with the needs of your children. You can't claim to always have done so gracefully, but you did it and it paid off.

After a little over a year of busting your ass at the marketing agency, you get recruited by one of the firm's clients, a philanthropic organization established by a local retired tech powerhouse. They want to take their marketing work in-house and ask you to come lead the team. This is the first time you have felt like someone has really seen your potential in a long time, and you cry that night as you tell Nathan the news.

The best part of your new job is your chance to build your small team from scratch. Not only do you get to find great candidates, but you feel like you have the opportunity to clear some of the barriers that you experienced when trying to reestablish yourself at work. With that in mind, you are very conscious of not letting biases get in the way of your resume screening or interviewing.

Your small team works great together, and the heads of the organization are happy with your work. You even get to hire a few more people as your work scales. You make it known that it is important for you to leave by five every day to have dinner with your kids, and no one questions that. You are doing great work, so why would they?

From time to time, other mothers at your kids' school ask you out to coffee for advice about how to rejoin the workforce. You don't sugar-coat it and let them know how brutal it can be. But you also give them encouragement to stick it out: both the job search and the reentry. After all, you did and are here to tell the story . . . and to live happily ever after being reestablished in the workforce.

The End

*(Want to see what would have happened if you had decided not to stick it out at work? Turn back to **Chapter 53** and make a different choice. Or if you've explored all the paths, turn to the **Epilogue**.)*

55

HAPPILY EVER AFTER
WITH A BFF

D r. Malone prescribes an antianxiety medication for you, which you start taking daily. It takes a couple of weeks for you to notice a difference, but when you do, it feels like you can take a full breath and think through a full idea for the first time in months. The sense of relief is palpable.

It takes a little longer for you to overcome the sense of embarrassment you feel for taking medication. You believe there is a stigma around it and that you would be thought of as "crazy" if anyone knew. Then one night at your book club, after a few glasses of wine (which hit you a bit harder than they used to, thanks to the medication), you admit to your friends that you started taking it. To your shock, three quarters of the women in the room are either on antianxiety medication or antidepressants or have been in the past. This sense of solidarity banishes your shame.

· · ·

Not long after this, you are driving home from work on your way to pick up Zoe and are thinking about how relieved you feel to not have the anxiety rushing through your veins any-more, and how lucky you are to have such a supportive group of friends who you can be vulnerable with. You are listening to the five o-clock flashback hour on the radio, and "Don't Stop Believing" comes on. You start singing along at the top of your lungs and don't see the sedan making a left turn through a yellow light. The car crashes into your passenger side door and your airbag releases.

As you lie in the hospital with two broken ribs and a black eye, the doctor tells you that no one else was badly hurt and you're very lucky that you're not worse off. You are in severe pain, but more than that, you feel terrified, thinking about what could have happened. When Silas brings Zoe to see you that night, you cry tears of relief as you hold her little hand in yours.

After your ribs heal, you start going to physical therapy and a chiropractor. You have been having back pain ever since the accident, and the fact that it is not getting better has you wor-ried. You know that motor vehicle accidents account for almost half of spinal injuries each year, and you meet two other people at your PT office who are dealing with similar issues.[1] One of them, a woman named Heather, also has a five-year-old daugh-ter. The two of you hit it off and decide to plan a playdate.

Years later, you still have intermittent discomfort in your back from your car accident. But you've learned some stretches that help you work through it and your pain tolerance is pretty high. And despite all of this, you can't bring yourself to wish the accident never happened. If that car hadn't hit you, you never would have met Heather. The two of you have become life-long friends, and your daughters grow up as close friends as well. You live happily ever after with some chronic pain and an amazing friend for life.

The End

(Want to see what would have happened if you had decided not to go on antianxiety medication? Turn back to Chapter 44 and make a different choice. Or if you've explored all the paths, turn to the Epilogue.)

56

MEDITATION

Since deciding not to medicate, you know you need to find some way to stop the panic attacks. After extensive internet research, you sign up for some mindfulness classes at a yoga studio down the street from your office. You start learning about breath work and meditation, both of which prove to be immensely valuable both in managing your anxiety and in helping you fall asleep at night.

You then start taking yoga classes there during your lunch hour. It is in one such class, after setting your intention to listen to your inner voice, that you have an epiphany: anxiety isn't inherent to you, it is something that your job is bringing out in you. This idea coalesces in your mind until you realize you need to do something about it. You start a job search.

As you do, you continue on to **Chapter 58**.

57

HAPPILY EVER AFTER BLENDING FAMILIES

You've started volunteering at a local food bank on Saturdays; it was one of the few such opportunities you found where you were able to bring Lily with you. The two of you separate out donated food and hygiene supplies and line them up on the shelves in the storeroom. Although you're not sure how much of a life lesson she is taking from the activity at the age of five, Lily does love the organizational aspect of it. You feel good that you're able to set a good example for her and give back to your community in a small way.

You are also saying yes to more of the fundraising and charity celebrations that your friends and colleagues invite you to. At one luncheon for an organization that provides STEM mentorship for underserved youth, you end up striking up a conversation with a friend of your colleague, a man named Patrick. You and Patrick are both moved by the presentation and decide to grab coffee afterwards to talk more about it. You can't lie to yourself: it wasn't just the presentation that has you interested in coffee with him. Patrick is handsome and interesting to talk to.

Patrick was the college roommate of your coworker who invited you to the luncheon. He is a recently divorced father of two who works in finance and plays racquetball on weekends. Although he is more preppy than your usual taste, the two of you have an immediate chemistry. You start getting a babysitter every other Saturday to go on dates with him, on the nights that he doesn't have his kids. As a single mother, you can't manage much more than that for a while, and you're not ready for him to meet Lily yet.

However, after several months of casual dating, you and Patrick decide that you really have feelings for each other. It's time to introduce your kids. Despite all of your worry over the introduction, Lily takes an immediate liking to Patrick. He builds a Lego castle with her and she's practically smitten.

• • •

Two years later, you and Patrick move in together. Lily is, of course, with you full-time and Patrick's two children, Bella and Mason, stay with you every other week. They are two and four years older than her, respectively. Although she needs some work to get used to sharing toys and attention, Lily loves having them to play with. They are like the 16 percent of children in the US living in a blended family.[1]

You continue to pay the minimum on your student loans and add an extra payment on when you're able. It takes longer than it might have, but fourteen years later, you are finally debt-free.

You and Patrick eventually end up deciding to get married. All three children, as well as your new puppy Oscar, are in the wedding. Your household is large and messy, and you wouldn't have it any other way. You live happily ever after as a blended family.

The End

(Want to see what would have happened if you had decided to pay your student loans back faster instead? Turn back to Chapter 40 and make a different choice. Or if you've explored all the paths, turn to the Epilogue.)

58

HAPPILY EVER AFTER INSPIRING OTHERS

You are able to do a job search in which you are not rushed and are adequately picky about where you land, which is a luxury compared to other times in your life. After a few informational interviews and some phone screenings, you end up interviewing for a communications manager role at an early education nonprofit. It is a shift from your current role, but it sounds like interesting and important work, and you like the idea of working somewhere less corporate. When they offer you the job, you negotiate the salary up to almost what you had been making and decide to take the leap.

The nonprofit ends up being a great fit for you. Several of your colleagues also have small children, so you don't feel self-conscious about the times you need to leave early or work from home in order to take care of Zoe. You are even able to stop paying for a nanny, which helps make up for the small salary decrease you had to take.

Without having to change who you are, you end up being promoted to director after less than two years. You feel calmer, less anxious, and more appreciated than you ever have in your career.

One drizzly Sunday afternoon, as you are pushing Zoe on the swings at the playground with your rain boots on and a mug of coffee in one hand, you overhear two moms talking next to the slides. One of them is complaining about how she keeps getting turned down for a promotion at work because she doesn't have enough "leadership traits." You can't help yourself—you have to interject.

You end up talking for an hour with these new friends about the unactionable personality feedback that holds women back at work. You tell them your story, and they are inspired by the career move you ended up making.

After a few subsequent coffee conversations, the three of you decide to form a Facebook group named "Calling Bullshit on Gender-Biased Reviews," in which women can share their stories of stifled career paths couched behind personality-based performance review feedback. You end up gaining more than 100,000 members in the first year and find the group to be a fulfilling and inspiring side project. You live happily ever after inspiring others to share their stories so you can lift each other up.

The End

(Want to see what would have happened if you had con-formed to a corporate professional norm instead? Turn back to Chapter 31 and make a different choice. Or if you've explored all the paths, turn to the Epilogue.)

EPILOGUE

By now, hopefully you have explored a number of different paths through some of the most pivotal years of your life. Although the parallel universes of outcomes in this book are varied, they are still only an infinitely small fraction of what you may actually experience. Whether or not your own trail mirrors any of these, my hope is that you come away from this book ready to face these or any other challenges and choices you encounter in your own life.

Although there were many endings in this book—all of them "happy" in their own way—none of them were truly endings. Life goes on with new sets of challenges and accomplishments, new beginnings, and life-altering relationships. The experiences that defined your 20s and 30s will give you the wisdom and strength to navigate these next chapters and blaze entirely new trails.

After exploring this book, I hope you feel confident that there is no one right choice you need to make—no singular path that you need to be following. Each decision you make will teach you new lessons, provide more opportunities from which to build strength, and hopefully, each will open your heart a little further. And remember, no matter how painful an outcome, or how preventable a path might appear in hindsight, as long as you are alive, you will make it through.

I hope you feel solidarity in knowing that every experience, no matter how lonely or embarrassing or isolating it feels in the moment, is one that countless other women have gone through, are going through, and will go through. There is a sisterhood in our traumas, a bond we can embrace throughout time and distance with so many others who share our experiences. If data is what moves you, then let the numbers provide you with solace to show you that you are not alone. And if stories resonate more, then share yours on owntrail.com and seek out others to provide that common thread.

Work on feeling compassion for others, knowing that everyone is blazing their own trail, making their own decisions, and working through their own consequences all the time. We can't know what every person is going through, but we can act with empathy and try to make the intersections where our paths cross be ones of ease. When we are able to make space for each other's experiences and show each other compassion and support, we all travel down our paths more smoothly.

This journey is not ending, only beginning. Move forward with confidence, solidarity, and compassion, and blaze your own trail.

NOTES

CHAPTER 1

1. Ariane Hegewisch, M.Phil., and Emma Williams-Baron, "The Gender Wage Gap: 2017 Earnings Differences by Race and Ethnicity," Institute for Women's Policy Research, March 7, 2018, https://iwpr.org/publications /gender-wage-gap-2017-race-ethnicity/.
2. Jeffrey J. Selingo, "Two-Thirds of College Grads Struggle to Launch Their Careers," *Harvard Business Review*, May 31, 2016, https://hbr.org/2016/05 /two-thirds-of-college-grads-struggle-to-launch-their-careers.
3. Mark Huffman, "Despite Low Unemployment, Many College Grads Are Out of Work," *Consumer Affairs*, June 18, 2018, https://www.consumeraffairs .com/news/despite-low-unemployment-many-college-grads-are-out-of -work-061818.html.

CHAPTER 4

1. "Millennials More Engaged In CSR, Study Says," *Holmes Report*, October 4, 2015, https://www.holmesreport.com/research/article/millennials-more -engaged-imn-csr-study-says.

CHAPTER 6

1. Egon Zehnder, "Leaders and Daughters Global Survey 2017," Egon Zehnder International, February 27, 2017, https://s3-eu-west-1.amazonaws .com/public-gbda/Leaders_Daughters_Final.pdf.
2. Benjamin Soskis, "When It Comes to Saving US Jobs, What About Non-profits?" Urban Institute, Urban Wire blog, June 25, 2017, https://www.urban .org/urban-wire/when-it-comes-saving-us-jobs-what-about-nonprofits.
3. T. J. Murphy, "How Many People Go to Graduate School and a Few Other Questions," Gradschoolmatch blog, March 12, 2017, http://blog .gradschoolmatch.com/people-going-graduate-school/.

CHAPTER 7

1. Danielle Page, "How Impostor Syndrome Is Holding You Back at Work," NBC Universal, October 25, 2017, https://www.nbcnews.com/better /health/how-impostor-syndrome-holding-you-back-work-ncna814231.
2. Alexis Krivkovich, Marie-Claude Nadeau, Kelsey Robinson, Nicole Robinson, Irina Starikova, and Lareina Yee, "Women in the Workplace 2018," McKinsey and Company, October 2018, https://www.mckinsey.com /featured-insights/gender-equality/women-in-the-workplace-2018#0.

CHAPTER 8

1. Chai R. Feldblum and Victoria A. Lipnic, "Select Task Force on the Study of Harassment in the Workplace," US Equal Employment Opportunity Commission, June 2016, https://www.eeoc.gov/eeoc /task_force/harassment/upload/report.pdf; Tara Golshan, "Study Finds 75 percent of Workplace Harassment Victims Experienced Retaliation When They Spoke Up," *Vox,* October 15, 2017, https://www.vox .com/identities/2017/10/15/16438750/weinstein-sexual-harassment -facts.

CHAPTER 9

1. "What Are the Odds of Getting Pregnant?" WebMD, from "Getting Started on Getting Pregnant," https://www.webmd.com/baby/qa/what-are-the -odds-of-getting-pregnant, accessed June 17, 2019.
2. "Abortion Is a Common Experience for U.S. Women, Despite Dramatic Declines in Rates," Guttmacher Institute, October 19, 2017, https://www .guttmacher.org/news-release/2017/abortion-common-experience-us -women-despite-dramatic-declines-rates.
3. "The Majority of Children Live with Two Parents, Census Bureau Reports," United States Census Bureau, November 17, 2016, https://www .census.gov/newsroom/press-releases/2016/cb16-192.html.

CHAPTER 11

1. Skylar Olsen, "Buy/Rent Breakeven: How Much Time Ya' Got?" Zillow, July 10, 2015, https://www.zillow.com/research/q1-2015-buy-rent -breakeven-10108/.
2. Zillow Research, "16 Favorite Facts from the Zillow Group Report on Consumer Housing Trends Report 2018," Zillow, September 26, 2018, https://www.zillow.com/research/zillow-group-report-2018-21447/.

CHAPTER 12

1. Rhitu Chatterjee, "A New Survey Finds 81 Percent of Women Have Experienced Sexual Harassment," NPR: The Two-Way, February 21, 2018, https://www.npr.org/sections/thetwo-way/2018/02/21/587671849/a-new-survey-finds-eighty-percent-of-women-have-experienced-sexual-harassment.
2. G. D. Rosenblum and L. S. Taska, "Self-Defense Training as Clinical Intervention for Survivors of Trauma," *Violence Against Women* 20, no. 3 (March 2014), 293-308, https://doi.org/10.1177/1077801214526048.

CHAPTER 13

1. Shannon Clark, "6 Surprising Stats That Will Change the Way You Give Birth,", Affording Motherhood blog, https://growingslower.com/surprising-birth-statistics/, accessed June 17, 2019.
2. BabyCenter Editorial Team, "What Are My Chances of Getting Through Labor without an Epidural?" BabyCenter, https://www.babycenter.com/404_what-are-my-chances-of-getting-through-labor-without-an-epid_10331102.bc, accessed June 17, 2019.

CHAPTER 14

1. Chris Taylor, "In Defense of the Courthouse Wedding," *Reuters,* May 21, 2015, https://www.reuters.com/article/us-money-wedding-courthouse/in-defense-of-the-courthouse-wedding-idUSKBN0O61OB20150521.
2. Associated Press, "Poll: Most Men Aspire to Be Dads," *USA Today,* June 15, 2013, https://www.usatoday.com/story/news/nation/2013/06/15/poll-most-men-aspire-to-be-dads/2427123/.
3. Seth Wynes and Kimberly A. Nicholas, "The Climate Mitigation Gap: Education and Government Recommendations Miss the Most Effective Individual Actions," *IOPScience,* Environmental Research Letters, July 12, 2017, http://iopscience.iop.org/article/10.1088/1748-9326/aa7541.

CHAPTER 15

1. Cathleen Clerkin, "What Women Want—And Why You Want Women—In the Workplace," July 2017, Center for Creative Leadership, https://www.ccl.org/wp-content/uploads/2017/07/WhatWomenWant.FINAL_.pdf.
2. LinkedIn Talent Solutions, "Why & How People Change Jobs," LinkedIn, 2015, https://business.linkedin.com/content/dam/business/talent-solutions/global/en_us/job-switchers/PDF/job-switchers-global-report-english.pdf.

3. Samantha McLaren, "5 Stats about Women in the Workforce That You Need to Know," LinkedIn Talent blog, July 5, 2017, https://business .linkedin.com/talent-solutions/blog/trends-and-research/2017/5-stats -about-women-in-the-workforce-that-you-need-to-know.

CHAPTER 16

1. Care.com Editorial Staff, "This Is How Much Child Care Costs in 2018," Care.com, July 17, 2018, https://www.care.com/c/stories/2423/how-much -does-child-care-cost/.
2. Kim Parker, "Women More Than Men Adjust Their Careers for Family Life," Pew Research Center, Factank: News in the Numbers, October 1, 2015, https://www.pewresearch.org/fact-tank/2015/10/01/women-more -than-men-adjust-their-careers-for-family-life/.

CHAPTER 17

1. "What Is Postpartum Depression & Anxiety?" American Psychological Association, https://www.apa.org/pi/women/resources/reports /postpartum-depression.aspx, accessed June 17, 2019.

CHAPTER 18

1. Kim Parker, "Despite Progress, Women Still Bear Heavier Load Than Men in Balancing Work and Family," Pew Research Center, Factank: News in the Numbers, March 10, 2015, http://www.pewresearch .org/fact-tank/2015/03/10/women-still-bear-heavier-load-than-men -balancing-work-family/.
2. A. W. Geiger, Gretchen Livingston, and Kristen Bialik, "6 Facts about U.S. Moms," Pew Research Center, Factank: News in the Numbers, May 8, 2019, https://www.pewresearch.org/fact-tank/2019/05/08/facts-about -u-s-mothers/.
3. Rose Leadem, "Is Work-Life Balance Even Possible?" *Entrepreneur*, February 18, 2018, https://www.entrepreneur.com/article/309121.
4. Parker, "Despite Progress."

CHAPTER 19

1. Brady E. Hamilton, Joyce A. Martin, Michelle J. K. Osterman, Anne K. Driscoll, and Lauren M. Rossen, "Births: Provisional Data for 2017," US Department of Health and Human Services: National Vital Statistics System, May 2018, https://www.cdc.gov/nchs/data/vsrr /report004.pdf.

2. MedlinePlus, "Reflux in Infants," National Institute of Health: US National Library of Medicine, https://medlineplus.gov/refluxininfants.html, accessed June 17, 2019.

3. Lisa Gatti, "Maternal Perceptions of Insufficient Milk Supply in Breast-feeding," *Journal of Nursing Scholarship,* November 25, 2008, https://doi.org/10.1111/j.1547-5069.2008.00234.x.

4. CDC, "Breastfeeding Data & Statistics," Centers for Disease Control and Prevention, https://www.cdc.gov/breastfeeding/data/facts.html, accessed June 17, 2019.

CHAPTER 20

1. Toni Weschler, Taking Charge of Your Fertility: The Definitive Guide to Natural Birth Control, Pregnancy Achievement, and Reproductive Health (William Morrow Paperbacks, 2015).

2. Jessica Kelmon, "How Long Does It Take to Get Pregnant?" BabyCenter, May 2017, https://www.babycenter.com/how-long-does-it-take-to-get-pregnant.

CHAPTER 21

1. A. W. Geiger, Gretchen Livingston, Kristen Bialik, "6 Facts about U.S. Moms," Pew Research Center, Factank: News in the Numbers, May 8, 2019, https://www.pewresearch.org/fact-tank/2019/05/08/facts-about-u-s-mothers/.

CHAPTER 22

1. Valentina Zarya, "The 2017 Fortune 500 Includes a Record Number of Women CEOs," *Fortune,* June 7, 2017, http://fortune.com/2017/06/07/fortune-women-ceos/.

CHAPTER 24

1. Claire Zillman, "Childcare Costs More Than College Tuition in 28 U.S. States," *Fortune,* October 22, 2018, http://fortune.com/2018/10/22/childcare-costs-per-year-us/.

2. Quoctrung Bui and Claire Cain Miller, "The Typical American Lives Only 18 Miles from Mom," *New York Times,* December 23, 2015, https://www.nytimes.com/interactive/2015/12/24/upshot/24up-family.html.

CHAPTER 26

1. "Intrauterine Insemination: IUI," American Pregnancy Association, Updated January 10, 2019, https://americanpregnancy.org/infertility/intrauterine-insemination/.

2. "In Vitro Fertilization: IVF," American Pregnancy Association, Updated January 10, 2019, https://americanpregnancy.org/infertility /in-vitro-fertilization/.

3. Guardian Press Association, "IVF Pregnancy Less Successful with Two Embryos, Study Finds," *Guardian,* January 4, 2017, https://www .theguardian.com/science/2017/jan/05/ivf-pregnancy-less-successful -with-two-embryos-study-finds.

4. Chandni Patel, "One IVF Pregnancy Raises Chance of Second Time Success," *BioNews,* September 25, 2017, https://www.bionews.org.uk/page _96186.

CHAPTER 27

1. Jessica Deahl, "Countries Around the World Beat the U.S. on Paid Parental Leave," NPR, October 6, 2016, https://www.npr.org/2016/10/06/495839588 /countries-around-the-world-beat-the-u-s-on-paid-parental-leave.

2. Ashley May, "Paid Family Leave Is an Elite Benefit in the U.S.," *USA Today,* May 17, 2017, https://www.usatoday.com/story/news/nation-now/2017/05 /17/paid-maternity-leave-elite-benefit-u-s/325075001/.

3. What to Expect Editors, "What to Do If Your Water Breaks During Pregnancy," What to Expect, April 26, 2019, https://www.whattoexpect.com /pregnancy/symptoms-and-solutions/water-breaking-during-pregnancy .aspx.

4. Belinda Luscombe, "No, All Those Strollers Aren't Your Imagination. More Women Are Having Children," *Time,* January 19, 2018, http://time .com/5107704/more-women-mothers/.

CHAPTER 28

1. Amelia Josephson, "The Cost of a Career Break," SmartAsset, December 26, 2016, https://smartasset.com/career/the-cost-of-a-career-break.

2. Wendy Wang, "Who Cheats More? The Demographics of Infidelity in America," Institute for Family Studies, January 10, 2018, https://ifstudies .org/blog/who-cheats-more-the-demographics-of-cheating-in-america.

CHAPTER 30

1. Niraj Chokshi, "Out of the Office: More People Are Working Remotely, Survey Says," *New York Times,* February 15, 2017, https://www.nytimes .com/2017/02/15/us/remote-workers-work-from-home.html.

2. Sarah Szczypinski, "The 'Happiness Gap': What Having Kids Really Does to Your Marriage," *Today*, June 27, 2017, https://www.today.com/parents/does-having-children-destroy-happy-marriage-t113028.

CHAPTER 31

1. Paola Cecchi-Dimeglio, "How Gender Bias Corrupts Performance Reviews, and What to Do about It," *Harvard Business Review*, April 12, 2017, https://hbr.org/2017/04/how-gender-bias-corrupts-performance-reviews-and-what-to-do-about-it.

CHAPTER 32

1. Glassdoor Team, "3 in 5 Employees Did Not Negotiate Salary," Glassdoor, May 2, 2016, https://www.glassdoor.com/blog/3-5-u-s-employees-negotiate-salary/.

CHAPTER 33

1. Claire Cain Miller and Derek Willis, "Maiden Names, on the Rise Again," *New York Times*, June 27, 2015, https://www.nytimes.com/2015/06/28/upshot/maiden-names-on-the-rise-again.html.
2. Robin Hilmantel, "How Men REALLY Feel When You Keep Your Last Name," *Women's Health*, August 8, 2013, https://www.womenshealthmag.com/relationships/a19903379/how-men-really-feel-when-you-keep-your-last-name/.

CHAPTER 34

1. "Get the Facts & Figures," The National Domestic Violence Hotline, accessed June 17, 2019, https://www.thehotline.org/resources/statistics/.

CHAPTER 36

1. Jane E. Brody, "When a Partner Cheats," *New York Times*, January 22, 2018, https://www.nytimes.com/2018/01/22/well/marriage-cheating-infidelity.html.
2. Gabrielle Applebury, "Rates of Divorce for Adultery and Infidelity," LoveToKnow Corp., https://divorce.lovetoknow.com/Rates_of_Divorce_for_Adultery_and_Infidelity, accessed June 17, 2019.

3. Kayla Knopp, Shelby Scott, Lane Ritchie, Galena K. Rhoades, Howard J. Markman, and Scott M. Stanley, "Once a Cheater, Always a Cheater? Serial Infidelity Across Subsequent Relationships," *Archives of Sexual Behavior, 46, 8* (2017), 2301–2311, https://link.springer.com/article/10.1007/s10508-017-1018-1.

CHAPTER 37

1. Shelby B. Scott, Galena K. Rhoades, Scott M. Stanley, Elizabeth S. Allen, and Howard J. Markman, "Reasons for Divorce and Recollections of Premarital Intervention: Implications for Improving Relationship Education," *Couple and Family Psychology: Research and Practice* 2, no. 2 (Jun 2013), 131–145https://psycnet.apa.org/doiLanding?doi=10.1037%2Fa0032025.
2. Gabrielle Applebury, "Rates of Divorce for Adultery and Infidelity," LoveToKnow Corp., https://divorce.lovetoknow.com/Rates_of_Divorce_for_Adultery_and_Infidelity, accessed June 17, 2019.
3. John Bingham, "Getting Married Before Having Children 'Boosts Chances of Staying Together'—Study," *Telegraph,* March 9, 2015, https://www.telegraph.co.uk/news/politics/11457510/Getting-married-before-having-children-boosts-chances-of-staying-together-study.html.

CHAPTER 39

1. Zawn Villines, "How Soon Can You Get Pregnant after Giving Birth?" *Medical News Today,* October 9, 2018, https://www.medicalnewstoday.com/articles/323286.php.
2. Sylvia Ann Hewlett and Carolyn Buck Luce, "Off-Ramps and On-Ramps: Keeping Talented Women on the Road to Success," *Harvard Business Review,* March 2005, https://hbr.org/2005/03/off-ramps-and-on-ramps-keeping-talented-women-on-the-road-to-success.

CHAPTER 40

1. Abigail Hess, "Here's How Much the Average Student Loan Borrower Owes When They Graduate," CNBC.com, Make It, February 15, 2018, https://www.cnbc.com/2018/02/15/heres-how-much-the-average-student-loan-borrower-owes-when-they-graduate.html; Abigail Hess, "This Is the Age Most Americans Pay Off Their Student Loans," CNBC.com, Make It, July 3, 2017, https://www.cnbc.com/2017/07/03/this-is-the-age-most-americans-pay-off-their-student-loans.html.
2. "Charitable Giving Statistics," National Philanthropic Trust, https://www.nptrust.org/philanthropic-resources/charitable-giving-statistics/,

accessed June 17, 2019; Una Osili and Sasha Zarins, "Fewer Americans Are Giving Money to Charity but Total Donations Are at Record Levels Anyway," *The Conversation,* July 3, 2018, https://theconversation.com /fewer-americans-are-giving-money-to-charity-but-total-donations-are -at-record-levels-anyway-98291.

CHAPTER 41

1. "Dementia," World Health Organization, May 14, 2019, https://www.who .int/en/news-room/fact-sheets/detail/dementia.
2. "Dementia," World Health Organization.
3. Richard Fry, "More Adults Now Share Their Living Space, Driven in Part by Parents Living with Their Adult Children," Pew Research Center, January 31, 2018, http://www.pewresearch.org/fact-tank/2018/01/31/more -adults-now-share-their-living-space-driven-in-part-by-parents -living-with-their-adult-children/.

CHAPTER 42

1. "Why Do Victims Stay?" National Coalition Against Domestic Violence, https://ncadv.org/why-do-victims-stay, accessed June 17, 2019.
2. Amari O'Bannon, "We Can No Longer Be Silent: How Intimate Partner Violence Affects Women of Color," July 7, 2016, National Organization of Women, https://now.org/blog/we-can-no-longer-be-silent-how-intimate -partner-violence-affects-women-of-color/.

CHAPTER 43

1. Richard Fry, "It's Becoming More Common for Young Adults to Live at Home—And for Longer Stretches," Pew Research Center, May 5, 2017, http://www.pewresearch.org/fact-tank/2017/05/05/its-becoming-more -common-for-young-adults-to-live-at-home-and-for-longer-stretches/.
2. Patrick Sisson, "How a Return to Multigenerational Living Is Shifting the Housing Market," *Curbed,* November 21, 2017, https://www .curbed.com/2017/11/21/16682850/multigenerational-homes-millennials -immigration-family.

CHAPTER 44

1. "About ADAA—Facts & Statistics," Anxiety and Depression Association of America, https://adaa.org/about-adaa/press-room/facts-statistics, accessed June 17, 2019.

CHAPTER 45

1. Nicole Lyn Pesce, "Nearly 44M Americans Are Unpaid Adult Caregivers," *New York Post*, July 20, 2018, https://nypost.com/2018/07/20/nearly-44m-americans-are-unpaid-adult-caregivers/.
2. Kim Parker and Eileen Patten, "The Sandwich Generation: Rising Financial Burdens for Middle-Aged Americans," Pew Research Center: Social and Demographic Trends, January 30, 2013, http://www.pewsocialtrends.org/2013/01/30/the-sandwich-generation/.

CHAPTER 46

1. "Data & Statistics on Autism Spectrum Disorder," Centers for Disease Control and Prevention, April 5, 2019, https://www.cdc.gov/ncbddd/autism/data.html.

CHAPTER 47

1. Rebecca A. Marín, Andrew Christensen, and David C. Atkins, "Infidelity and Behavioral Couple Therapy: Relationship Outcomes Over 5 Years Following Therapy," Couple and *Family Psychology: Research and Practice* 3, 1–12 (2014), https://www.apa.org/pubs/journals/features/cfp-0000012.pdf.

CHAPTER 48

1. "1900–2000: Changes in Life Expectancy in the United States," Senior Living.org, https://www.seniorliving.org/history/1900-2000-changes-life-expectancy-united-states/, accessed June 17, 2019.
2. "Alzheimer's Association Releases Dementia Care Practice Recommendations for End-of-Life Care," Alzheimer's Association, August 28, 2007, https://www.alz.org/national/documents/release_082807_dcrecommends.pdf.

CHAPTER 49

1. Denise Erlich, "Single Fathers, Single Mothers, and Child Custody Statistics," Erlich Law Office blog, https://erlichlegal.com/blog/single-fathers-single-mothers-child-custody-statistics/, accessed June 17, 2019.
2. Richard A. Warshak, "After Divorce, Shared Parenting Is Best for Children's Health and Development," Stat News, May 26, 2017, https://www.statnews.com/2017/05/26/divorce-shared-parenting-children-health/.

CHAPTER 53

1. Sylvia Ann Hewlett and Carolyn Buck Luce, "Off-Ramps and On-Ramps: Keeping Talented Women on the Road to Success," March 2005, *Harvard Business Review,* https://hbr.org/2005/03/off-ramps-and-on-ramps -keeping-talented-women-on-the-road-to-success.

CHAPTER 55

1. "Coping with Chronic Pain after a Car Accident," Apex Medical Center blog, https://www.apexmedicalcenter.com/blog/managing-chronic-pain -after-a-car-accident, accessed June 17, 2019.

CHAPTER 57

1. "The American Family Today," Pew Research Center: Social and Demographic Trends, December 17, 2015, https://www.pewsocialtrends.org /2015/12/17/1-the-american-family-today/.

ACKNOWLEDGMENTS

This book took several months to write, but forty years to prepare for. I wouldn't have had the journeys that I have had, or the amazing experience of publishing a book, without the partnership of many people who helped me find my own confidence, solidarity, and compassion.

I must first thank my parents, Bette and Richard, as they were the first people to instill in me the understanding that there is no one right path, and that I am strong enough to make it through any obstacles. Admittedly, they also let me skip over the scary parts in my childhood books, which might have biased me toward happy endings. But the way they have always believed in me—even when I was doing my best to convince them otherwise—has given me the confidence to find my own "happily ever after" in many different forms.

My husband, Shane, is the other person who has believed in me tirelessly, since the day I looked up from my bartending job and made eye contact with him back in 2001. He once told me that he loves me because I don't know what's not possible. That love is what has given me the confidence to keep choosing the paths that look too steep to climb.

My group at Zillow, the Community & Culture team, gives me confidence and inspiration every single day. In fact, the first people I told about my book idea were two of my teammates, after I woke up that morning with the idea in my head.

Jackie said "that's beautiful," and Lydia said "that's dope," and that was all I needed to hear to give it a shot! My manager Dan has been so supportive of my writing along with allowing me to forge my own career path. And my team was right there with me when I found out I had gotten a publishing deal with Berrett-Koehler; they dropped everything to have a champagne toast with me.

Speaking of Berrett-Koehler, I have had the most positive experience publishing with them. My editor, Anna, is now a friend for life—she completely gets where I am coming from, and her contributions to this book have made it what it is. The entire team there has been so supportive, and I love that they lead with transparency, community-building, and making the world better through the books that they publish. I hope this one lives up to that goal!

The love and vulnerability I have shared with close friends has been what has given me the solidarity to believe that none of us are alone on our journeys. My BFF, JJ, has been through everything with me for almost twenty years now. Annie and I have spent countless hours laughing and crying together. Lisa goes deep with me on every topic imaginable. My little sister, Nina, shares memories and perspectives with me that can only come from a shared childhood. The Wino Book Club has been an amazing source of solidarity, in addition to being my first beta readers for *Blaze Your Own Trail*. And the community at Versatile Arts, where I do aerial acrobatics, has been the most supportive and intimate environment in which to pursue my creative passions.

Finally, my biggest thanks go to the two people who have expanded my capacity for compassion beyond what I thought possible. My two sons, Max and Arlo, continue to open me up to a new level of love and awe. Becoming a mother changed my entire perspective of the world—it made me start seeing everyone as somebody's baby, and that inspires me to want to lead with love and empathy. My boys grace me with unbridled emotions, absurd humor, scientific explorations, music, trivia, art, play, and really good snuggles. And they've even made me become adept at pitching a Wiffle Ball! My gratitude for being their mother, and for the tenderness it has opened up in me, is without measure.

ABOUT THE AUTHOR

 Rebekah Bastian is a corporate culture leader, tech executive, writer, artist, speaker, mentor, wife, mother, and aerial acrobat. She has held leadership roles including vice president of product and vice president of community and culture at Zillow and cofounder and CEO of OwnTrail.

Rebekah serves as an advisor to tech startups and on several nonprofit boards. She is a contributor at Forbes.com and is a frequent speaker at conferences and community events. She has been recognized in the Puget Sound Business Journal 40 Under 40, the Inman 33 People Changing the Real Estate Industry, and the Female Founders Alliance Champion Awards.

Rebekah earned her Master's of Mechanical Engineering from the University of California Berkeley and her Bachelor's of Mechanical Engineering from the University of Washington. She lives in Seattle, WA, with her husband and two sons. Her path has never been linear or predictable, and she loves it that way.

Berrett–Koehler
Publishers

Berrett-Koehler is an independent publisher dedicated to an ambitious mission: *Connecting people and ideas to create a world that works for all.*

Our publications span many formats, including print, digital, audio, and video. We also offer online resources, training, and gatherings. And we will continue expanding our products and services to advance our mission.

We believe that the solutions to the world's problems will come from all of us, working at all levels: in our society, in our organizations, and in our own lives. Our publications and resources offer pathways to creating a more just, equitable, and sustainable society. They help people make their organizations more humane, democratic, diverse, and effective (and we don't think there's any contradiction there). And they guide people in creating positive change in their own lives and aligning their personal practices with their aspirations for a better world.

And we strive to practice what we preach through what we call "The BK Way." At the core of this approach is *stewardship,* a deep sense of responsibility to administer the company for the benefit of all of our stakeholder groups, including authors, customers, employees, investors, service providers, sales partners, and the communities and environment around us. Everything we do is built around stewardship and our other core values of *quality, partnership, inclusion,* and *sustainability.*

This is why Berrett-Koehler is the first book publishing company to be both a B Corporation (a rigorous certification) and a benefit corporation (a for-profit legal status), which together require us to adhere to the highest standards for corporate, social, and environmental performance. And it is why we have instituted many pioneering practices (which you can learn about at www.bkconnection.com), including the Berrett-Koehler Constitution, the Bill of Rights and Responsibilities for BK Authors, and our unique Author Days.

We are grateful to our readers, authors, and other friends who are supporting our mission. We ask you to share with us examples of how BK publications and resources are making a difference in your lives, organizations, and communities at www.bkconnection.com/impact.

Dear reader,

Thank you for picking up this book and welcome to the worldwide BK community! You're joining a special group of people who have come together to create positive change in their lives, organizations, and communities.

What's BK all about?

Our mission is to connect people and ideas to create a world that works for all.

Why? Our communities, organizations, and lives get bogged down by old paradigms of self-interest, exclusion, hierarchy, and privilege. But we believe that can change. That's why we seek the leading experts on these challenges—and share their actionable ideas with you.

A welcome gift

To help you get started, we'd like to offer you a **free copy** of one of our bestselling ebooks:

www.bkconnection.com/welcome

When you claim your **free ebook**, you'll also be subscribed to our blog.

Our freshest insights

Access the best new tools and ideas for leaders at all levels on our blog at ideas.bkconnection.com.

Sincerely,

Your friends at Berrett-Koehler